Adam Smith's Sociability and the American Dream

Adam Smith's Sociability and the American Dream

John E. Hill

LEXINGTON BOOKS
Lanham • Boulder • New York • London

Published by Lexington Books
An imprint of The Rowman & Littlefield Publishing Group, Inc.
4501 Forbes Boulevard, Suite 200, Lanham, Maryland 20706
www.rowman.com

86-90 Paul Street, London EC2A 4NE

British Library Cataloguing in Publication Information Available

Library of Congress Cataloging-in-Publication Data

Names: Hill, John E., 1942- author.
Title: Adam Smith's sociability and the American dream / John E. Hill.
Description: Lanham : Lexington Books, [2024] | Includes bibliographical references and index. | Summary: "Adam Smith's sociable market has been contorted into a free market; Christian love has become selfish individualism; John Adams' fear that elite domination would destroy our republic has been ignored. These three economic, religious, and political mistakes make it impossible for many to attain the American dream"-- Provided by publisher.
Identifiers: LCCN 2024012980 | ISBN 9781666946826 (cloth) | ISBN 9781666946833 (ebook)
Subjects: LCSH: Smith, Adam, 1723-1790. | Capitalism--Social aspects. | Free enterprise. | American dream. | United States--Economic conditions.
Classification: LCC HB103.S6 H55 2024 | DDC 330.15/3--dc23/eng/20240509
LC record available at https://lccn.loc.gov/2024012980

For Jeannette

Contents

Acknowledgments

It took a community to complete this book, and I was blessed with a talented community of family, friends, and colleagues. My sister, Elizabeth Cutting, and brother, Samuel Hill, were consistently supportive with their encouragement and suggestions. The manuscript also benefitted from Ronald Williams's expertise. Friends provided much-needed support at various stages in the process. The late Festus Ohaegbulam devoted significant time to an early draft, providing a helpful analysis; he was a true friend and an inspiration. Thomas P. Byrne III and Si Pearman responded with speed and grace to requests for assistance. Arthur Eisenkraft went beyond the call of duty with aid. Anonymous reviewers deserve more than a few words of appreciation; while some of their points were difficult to read, their critiques led to significant improvements in the manuscript.

Many colleagues also provided support. Leslie Becker, Katharine Eastman, and other librarians at the Levin Library at Curry College responded efficiently and with good humor to my requests. Chris Swenson rapidly and clearly answered my computer questions. Melissa Anyiwo, Grant Burrier, and others were always encouraging. Thomas P. Byrne Jr. read various drafts; his observations were trenchant and his life a model to be emulated. W. Russell Pregeant has always been a kindred spirit; this work has been enriched by our collaboration over the years. Larry Hartenian believed in this project from the beginning, often asking important questions and making valuable comments.

Finally, Jeannette DeJong, my wife, best friend, and persistent editor made certain that my awkward phraseology and overuse of certain words and phrases were minimized. Any errors that her eagle eyes overlooked are my responsibility entirely.

It took a village to complete this work.

Introduction

"Nightmare" describes the American Dream today. While the wealthy live lives of luxury, the middle and working classes struggle to survive. Why has the dream turned sour? This book is based on the assumption that capitalism, Christianity, and democracy are fundamental aspects of American society, but that society is not flourishing because most Americans, assuming their actions conform to these three fundamentals, misconstrue them. John Adams's fear of a lethal virus in democracy was not appreciated; his warnings about the dangers of aristocracy were ignored. This class has been able to dominate because the sociable and ethical market economy of Adam Smith has not been understood. His ideal was not a free market—the goal of market fundamentalists—but a sociable market with justice, liberty, and equality. Smith argued that increased productivity due to the division of labor made it possible to diffuse wealth to every socioeconomic class. Misunderstanding Adams and Smith has been made worse by an important third source of error: religion. Too often Christ's second commandment to love your neighbor as yourself is given only lip service; this mistake is made worse by a tendency to ignore who our neighbor is. The combined impact of these mistakes has caused this nightmare.

By labeling these mistakes, the author has no intention of pointing an accusatory finger at any one person; he is not a detective searching for the culprit. But these misinterpretations have combined to undermine the ideals of the founding generation, such as the equal right to life, liberty, and the pursuit of happiness in the Declaration of Independence.

Why has that dream of equal opportunity faded? Why is it that individualistic free market capitalism has enriched billionaires while the middle and working classes struggle with stagnant incomes? One significant change is that, while in the mid-twentieth century productivity increases were shared by all classes, more recently the gains have been monopolized by the wealthy. Specific policies that have contributed to the obscene growth of inequality, such as deindustrialization and tax reductions that largely benefit the wealthy, have a deeper cause: our capitalism is a hideous distortion of the sociable, just, and equal capitalism advocated by Smith. But capitalism *per se* has not caused global warming or the opioid crisis; as Naomi Oreskes and Erik Conway point out, "The culprit is market fundamentalist ideology, which denies capitalism's failures and refuses to endorse the best tool we have to address those failures, which is democratic government" (Oreskes and Conway 2023, 12).

Those sentences might cause you to think this work is a diatribe against capitalism and wealth; it is not. The author recognizes the efficacy of capitalism and that all classes made this country what it is. But he is critical of free market capitalism, advocating instead Smith's sociable capitalism. The book is aimed at Americans of all classes, as a reminder that we are all Americans. As our founders stated in the Declaration of Independence, we are all created equal, endowed with inalienable rights. But in the last half century, increasing individualism has weakened social bonds and thus undermined community, has made it more difficult for many to pursue their idea of a good life, and has weakened the economy.

How do free market capitalism (market fundamentalism) and sociable capitalism differ? Adam Smith did advocate a free market in international trade, but his arguments have been misinterpreted to include free domestic markets as well. However, what is good for international trade is not necessarily good for national markets. He advocated market economies, but within the parameters of his justice, liberty, and equality formula for "the highest degree of prosperity to all the three classes" (Smith 1789, III 13). His formula has been truncated to liberty alone, omitting justice and equality, thereby enabling a few to amass immense wealth. So the ideas of "the father of capitalism" are the foundation for market economies. But the irony is that existing market economies are gross distortions of the markets he envisioned.

The economic system that the revered Adam Smith advocated was not a free market, but a market shaped by the sociability of the "Impartial Spectator"—the central concept of his first book, *The Theory of Moral Sentiments,* in which he wrote that people act in ways they perceive an unbiased observer would approve. As Oreskes and Conway put it, Smith's philosophy is about counterbalancing "self-interest in economic activities with morality in guiding society." He argued "that self-interest is but one part of our instinctual apparatus; another equally important part is our capacity for empathy. Morality is rooted in concern for others, which is as much a part of our nature as self-interest is" (Oreskes and Conway 2023, 253–54). This gives society and the economy a sociable base, in contrast to the individualism so common today.

Though not explicitly mentioned in *Wealth of Nations*, the sociability of the impartial spectator was an underlying concept in that book. Smith's ideal market economy was characterized by sociability as well as justice, liberty, and equal opportunity. His understanding of individuality placed it firmly within communities. The people in his economy were not rugged individualists; they were sociable beings, individuals within communities. His sociability is understood by Smith scholars but contrasts with what many economists believe.

For centuries, most economists have not appreciated the importance of the impartial spectator from *Theory of Moral Sentiments* for understanding *Wealth of Nations*. Combine that omission with the missing equality and justice elements and one has a call for liberty alone. The resulting individualistic liberty means that we do not have the sociable market that he advocated.

Economists promoted individual self-interest at the expense of Smith's impartial spectator. His sociability places ethical boundaries on economies and thus is incompatible with free market individualism. A sociable market would still be a market economy, but it would be a fairer market. Chapter 2 develops this argument.

A sociable market economy would be consistent with other aspects of American society. Sociability is integral to Christianity (which was so important in the founding of this nation) and to other religions as well. This brings us to the second mistake. Christianity is often practiced individualistically, forgetting the love ethic of the great commandments. This is the focus of Chapter 3.

The third misinterpretation, the subject of Chapter 4, has deep historical roots. Most, if not all, of the founders misunderstood John Adams's warning that the "aristocracy" was dangerous to a democratic republic. Many thought he was advocating an aristocracy for the new nation; they misunderstood his repeated warnings that the aristocrats were major factors in the destruction of many democratic republics throughout history. Based on his extensive reading about republics through the centuries, he argued that they were fragile and easily overpowered by the aristocrats (his label for elites). He saw the aristocracy as "the greatest threat to political stability in any society" and thought its "essential foundation" was "control of large amounts of property" (Ryerson 2016, 311). He wanted our new system to protect against that danger and criticized it as inadequate to prevent such an elite coup. What he feared has happened. Elites have amassed immense wealth and use that wealth to dominate politics; the political power enables them to protect and increase their wealth.

Democracy is a perennial ideal—something a society should always be striving to perfect—but given the fallibility of humans can probably never be attained in its ideal form. Our founders bequeathed us this great ideal, but many of them did not appreciate how difficult it would be to implement and maintain. However, John Adams certainly understood, as is demonstrated by his writings on the dangers of factionalism and aristocracy.

Adams was a unique individual enmeshed in communities; he is included here, but not as a representative of a consensual political philosophy of the Founders. Far from it! He was a distinct person, as were the others, but they shared a concern for communities. They were certainly not a homogenous group of communitarians, nor were they rugged individualists; they had disagreements, but they believed in democracy (in its republican form). Emphasis on community is consistent with their thought. Adams's maligned warning that the elite are dangerous to democracy exemplifies his community concern; I focus on him for that reason, knowing full well that most, if not all, of the Founders did not understand his fear and therefore did not build any safeguards into the new governing system.

These three misinterpretations combined have contributed to an increase in individualism, at the expense of sociability, community, and the pursuit of happiness. But, while this book is a critique of individualism, it advocates individuality. It places the individual firmly within multiple communities, thereby strengthening both the individual and community.

Benefits of community are the subject of Chapter 5, which is not intended as a complete listing, but will focus instead on how it strengthens the economy. Chapter 6 examines connections between sociability and happiness. The final chapter examines some examples of community in the United States and makes some suggestions on future steps.

INDIVIDUALITY AND SOCIABILITY

We are individuals, but with myriad community connections. Our individuality can be seen in the unique combination of our connections, such as family, neighbors, town, work, clubs, church. The experiences we have with diverse groups shape us into unique individuals. As different communities leave their imprint, we are distinguished from each other. We are BOTH individuals AND members of communities. Keep this in mind as you read this work; if you read with an "either-or" mindset, you will grossly misinterpret the "both-and" argument.

The author's "both-and" mindset has been shaped by decades of reading, teaching, and reflecting on the state of the nation—and by statistics such as these, from the Social Progress Imperative organization, which "rigorously measures country performance on many aspects of social and environmental performance" (Green 2022, 3). In 2021, its index ranked the United States only twenty-fourth in the world; sadly, the United States has significantly declined in the last decade (Green 2022, 2 and 7). Many citizens will not be surprised by that ranking; they understand this country has not fulfilled the promises of our Founders.

Our history suggests a way to improve. In stressful times (such as the Revolutionary War, wartime in general, the Great Depression) we have pulled together for the greater good—we have been individuals within communities, sociable, not individualistic. But, the reader objects, this nation was founded based on individual liberty. Yes, liberty was among the founding principles, but within a community context. The word individualism was not used until the mid-nineteenth century (Barker-Benfield 2010, 291). Individualism would not have been viewed positively and would not have won independence; communities of individuals from multiple colonies worked together to win the right to life, liberty, and the pursuit of happiness. Victory in the Revolutionary War established an independent nation, a community of communities.

That two chapters deal with eighteenth-century figures and one with an ancient religion does not mean that I am yearning to return to some golden age. This book is written because we as a nation are not maximizing our potential for a better future for all; the American Dream is a dream for all Americans, not just the wealthy and well-connected. And the inclusiveness of that dream is consistent with the thought of Smith and Adams, and with Christianity.

A way of thinking and living that combines individuality with communities has been the source of our prosperity as a nation. But for most of our history, many members of the community—First Nations, African Americans, women, the poor—have been effectively denied the chance to reach their potential and share in the full benefits of community. While there has been some progress in recent decades, inequality persists. We have fallen far short of our ideals; at times, we have regressed. National wealth has grown, but it has become more concentrated at the top; the result is that more people are excluded from living the good life.

Bill McKibben explains what that exclusion means for many Americans: in addition to economic effects, people are less trusting, less likely to be civically engaged, and less happy. In addition, "epidemiologists tell us that the rise in economic inequality produced greater numbers of prisoners and school dropouts, more pregnant teenagers and drug users, far more mentally ill and obese people" (McKibben 2022, 175).

One reason the American dream has faded is increasing individualism, which McKibben labels hyperindividualism (McKibben 2022, 22 and 118). As Richard Haass notes, "Rugged individualism . . . is clearly on the upswing in this country. The problem is that it can all too easily descend into selfishness . . . if we fail to balance individual rights with obligations and our personal freedom with the public good . . . everyone loses" (Haass 2023, 116). And excessive individualism is counterproductive, as Robert Frank notes, "In many situations the conscious pursuit of self-interest is incompatible with its attainment" (Frank 1988, ix). Health, economic, and happiness metrics would all be better in this country if our society were characterized by individuality within communities.

Individualism harms our society, is contrary to our interests, and conflicts with our fundamental values, but the reader may be confused that I also argue for individuality within communities. It may sound like a contradiction, but it is not. More sociable people are happier and live fulfilling lives. To empower all individuals with real opportunities to attain their personal dream, we need to recognize that "individuality within communities" calls for an inclusive way of thinking, rejecting "either-or" thinking. This is an argument against excessive individualism, tribalism, and exclusion, not an argument to destroy individuality. There is no desire to impose conformity on anyone; this is a plea for sociability, a plea for a balance of individuality within strengthened and inclusive communities.

The author's dialectical, "both-and" thinking has been shaped by Gandhian ideas. Dialectical thinking results in a synthesis of thesis and antithesis. We are not limited to a choice between individuality or communities; we are individuals within multiple communities. Similarly, Gandhian thinking is "a dynamic end-creating method" (Bondurant 1971, 147). The goal of *Satyagraha* (Gandhi's "soul-force," directed at resolving an issue) is not the triumph of one side in a struggle but is a "synthesis of the two opposing claims" (Bondurant 1971, 196). Individuality within communities is the synthesis at the heart of this work. Individualism and excessive community are criticized; but individuality within communities is the goal.

Another way to explain my thinking is that it is influenced by the process relational school of thought. Russell Pregeant, a process relational theologian, writes about self-realization and self-transcendence, which can be called mutuality: "To have genuine mutuality as one's goal is not to abandon the quest for individuated selfhood but to seek the development of a self that exists in relation to other selves" (Pregeant 2022, 142). Individually, we have multiple connections with others within diverse communities. Humans are sociable beings.

This book emphasizes that we are a nation of many overlapping communities. Humans are not isolated atoms but members of diverse groups—family, neighborhood, work, among others—culminating in overarching communities, the city, the state, the nation, and ultimately the entire world. We are individuals existing in a multitude of interconnected groups. The author is convinced that "either-or" thinking impoverishes life; "individuality within communities" enriches life for all. But individualists worry that community stifles personal liberty. For instance, George Orwell's *1984* illustrates the danger of too much community destroying individual freedom. There is real tension between the two. Recognizing this danger, a balance of individuality within communities is important to prevent destruction of liberty. The good life is a perpetual quest to balance the two.

However, the problem now is not excessive community but excessive individualism. The unlimited individualism of our current casino capitalism privileges the wealthy while the other classes struggle. Liberty should not be dependent on socioeconomic class.

Extreme individualists are turning our capitalist system into a casino for high rollers alone, using their financial clout to subvert America's democracy and eliminating any chance for an equal opportunity society in which each person can develop to their fullest potential. If that seems too bleak a thought, note that John Adams feared the governmental dysfunction we are currently experiencing.

Perhaps this author has read too many of John Adams's warnings of the dangers to democratic republics; but his fears were based on the history of multiple democratic failures. While his contemporaries did not understand his concern, a modern author, Haass, does: "The United States has been around for close to two and a half centuries, but entities that were far older no longer exist, the consequence of the loss of a commitment to the whole that took precedence over the particular" (Haass 2023, 25).

In addition, two threads are implicit throughout this entire work; racism and sexism are significant impediments to a good society. Both are forms of exclusion. Both inhibit the development of strong individuals within healthy communities.

CONCLUSION

A word of caution: if you read this book *either* from an individualistic perspective *or* a community perspective, you will not understand it. The argument is against both excessive individualism and excessive community. For the remainder of this work, the reader should make a conscious effort to replace the "either-or" thinking that has been dominant in the West since at least the Greeks with "both-and" thinking. This will not be easy for those long habituated to "either-or" thinking. Readers would also miss the point if they overemphasize community. They would miss the creative tension of the sociable interaction of individuals within communities. Life is more fulfilling at that sweet spot, in contrast to the impoverished life of "one or the other."

To clarify its main purpose, this work aims to show that mistaken interpretations of Adam Smith, Christianity, and John Adams have thwarted the American Dream. Individuality within communities is consistent with American political-economic and religious values; greater sociability would revivify the quest for an equal right to life, liberty, and the pursuit of happiness for all Americans. Since the Declaration of Independence, this country has oscillated between more and less democratic governance. Since the 1970s, excessive individualism has transmuted our government into a plutocratic aristocracy. Returning to a democratic trajectory is long overdue. For that to happen, it is imperative that individuality within communities replace individualism; this would have the additional benefit of increasing happiness, given that scholars have shown the importance of social relations for happiness.

This yin-yang of individuality within communities is also consistent with the sociable market system advocated by Adam Smith, with Christianity, and with the values of the revolutionary generation. Individuality within communities is an ideal worth striving for. It would increase opportunities to pursue the American dream and strengthen the economy. Let us now examine this dialectical issue of individuality and community, and then move on to the mistaken interpretations of Smith, Christianity, and Adams.

Chapter One

Too Individualistic

Lost on the Road to Happiness

Excessive individualism is incompatible with democracy, impedes the pursuit of happiness, undermines the American dream, ignores the Christian love ethic, and contradicts Adam Smith who instead emphasized the importance of human sociability.

Readers who assume that individualism is the essence of Americanism will find that sentence incomprehensible, but bear with me as I explain. Democracy and the pursuit of happiness are enhanced by individuality within communities but weakened by individualism. Human societies cannot be democratic, cannot reach their economic potential, and cannot maximize happiness if many people exist for themselves alone. But individuals with multiple vibrant social relationships make for stronger communities. The issue is not "individuals" or "communities"; we need both in order to maximize opportunities for everyone to thrive. This theme pervades this entire work; reading this work with that in mind is imperative for understanding it.

"BOTH-AND": A SHORT HISTORY

Humanity has survived through millennia because of community: "Human beings have been practicing mutualism in every century on every continent, for as long as society has existed" (Horowitz 2021, 45). Bea Boccalandro found that our prehistoric ancestors were "noncompetitive, nonviolent and supportive of each other" (Boccalandro 2021, 156). Humans survived through prehistoric ages because of community. And so did the first settlers at Plymouth; they were cooperators, not individualists. While anchored off Cape Cod, and before landing at Plymouth, male passengers individually signed a community agreement. It should be noted that not all were Pilgrims, but they all signed an agreement to work together.

The Mayflower Compact was a mutual covenant to "combine together into a civill body politick, for our better ordering and preservation"; and the signatories agreed to regulate themselves "for the generall good of the colonie unto which we promise all due submission and obedience" (Mayflower Compact). All the passengers, men and women, had to be strong individuals to brave the Atlantic passage and establish a new colony (in northern Virginia, they thought). But they recognized that they would succeed or fail as a community. The community survived because individuals cooperated with one another and because of life-saving support from the indigenous peoples who had lived on the land long before they arrived. This illustrates the breadth of the community concept the author is using in this work; it includes the people already living in the New World, groups later vilified and driven nearly to extinction.

Community, rather than individualism, is important in our hallowed founding documents. For instance, promoting the general welfare is in the preamble to the US Constitution. Our Founders, of course, had no conception of contemporary welfare systems, but they believed government had a responsibility for the well-being (happiness) of all citizens, which is what the "general" in "general welfare" meant. The entire US Constitution is, of course, about the good of the community, but note that promoting the general welfare is emphasized by placing it in the preamble. This idea is a direct descendent of the equal right to pursue happiness, a common concern of Enlightenment thinkers on both sides of the Atlantic Ocean, and given equal billing along with life and liberty in the Declaration of Independence. Jefferson specifically argued "that the 'care of human life and happiness and not their destruction is the first and only legitimate object of good government'" (Oreskes and Conway 2023, 405).

John Quincy Adams understood this community orientation. Invited to give the 1802 annual oration celebrating the landing at Plymouth, he said the settlers remind us that "'Man was not made for himself alone.' The social compact binds the person to his country; the Christian obligation of 'universal charity' links the individual to other human beings" (Traub 2016, 119). Unfortunately, "universal charity" did not include Amerindians.

As Robert Putnam notes, Alexis de Tocqueville appreciated Americans' individual streak but recognized that they also valued community: "Through associating widely and deeply, they [Americans] were able to overcome selfish desires, engage in collective problem solving, and work together to build a vibrant and—by comparison to Europe at that time—surprisingly egalitarian society by pursuing what he called 'self-interest, rightly understood'" (Putnam 2020, 1–2). He later clarifies when he writes that "individuals' freedom to pursue their own interests holds great promise, but relentlessly exercising that freedom at the expense of others has the power to unravel the very foundations of the society that guarantees it" (Putnam

2020, 19). "Individuality within communities" is, then, people acting in their self-interest (individuality), while aware that working with others often promotes self-interest.

According to Putnam, Herbert Hoover "coined the term 'rugged individualism,'" in *American Individualism*, published in 1923, in which he "argued for a paradoxical blend of individualism and communitarianism" (Putnam 2020, 173). That combination may seem paradoxical, but it has been a foundation of our society.

Another Adams understood the "both-and" nature of our founding and development. In *The Epic of America*, written in the early 1930s, James Truslow Adams (not a descendent of Abigail and John) put a name on the phenomenon that had existed since the first settlers: "The *American dream* . . . is not a dream of motor cars and high wages merely but a dream of a social order in which each man and each woman shall be able to attain to the fullest stature of which they are innately capable, and be recognized by others for what they are, regardless of the fortuitous circumstances of birth or position" (Adams 1932, 404).

This definition may sound like an endorsement of individualism, not community, but community was an integral part of James Truslow Adams's understanding of the dream:

> The point is that if we are to have a rich and full life in which all are to share and play their parts, if the American dream is to be a reality, our communal spiritual and intellectual life must be distinctly higher than elsewhere, where classes and groups have their separate interests, habits, markets, arts, and lives. . . . We cannot become a great democracy by giving ourselves up as individuals to selfishness, physical comfort, and cheap amusements. (Adams 1932, 411)

His thinking was "both-and."

Our national motto for more than two centuries, "*E pluribus unum*" (Out of Many, One), might help clarify our "both-and" nature. Some might question the "pluribus": were we not one people? That seems plausible for the Mayflower Compact signatories, but more careful analysis shows they had significant differences. Some emigrated for religious freedom, others for economic reasons. Some immigrants brought theological disagreements; remember Roger Williams and Anne Hutchinson were exiled from Massachusetts Bay. Of course, religious conformity was maintained for a time by expelling these apostates (apostates, not from Christianity, but from a particular sect). But as more ships crossed the North Atlantic, more diverse immigrants arrived.

There were limits to community; the Amerindian residents of what was to become New England were excluded. Many were killed in King Philip's

War (the first of numerous genocidal actions against the First Nations), even though they had saved the settlers from death by starvation that first winter in the rugged wilderness. Two years before the Pilgrims landed at Plymouth, the first slaves arrived in Virginia, enabling plantation owners (and businessmen throughout the country, including New England) to develop luxurious lifestyles on the backs of human beings, viciously ripped from their African homes.

In the century and a half from the landing at Plymouth to Independence Day, all sorts of "others" came to the colonies: pacifist Quakers who would not fight for the king, and, even worse, Catholics. Twenty-first century Americans may have forgotten the animus toward those Romish peoples—supposedly slaves to the Pope. But as recently as John F. Kennedy's presidential campaign, that canard was used as a political weapon.

Americans are suffering from a bad case of amnesia; too many have forgotten the importance of community in establishing this nation. The amazing feat of winning independence from Great Britain, the strongest imperial power in the eighteenth century, was not accomplished by individualists; it required teamwork and widely shared sacrifice (plus a very important alliance with France and significant financial support from the Netherlands).

A sports analogy may help here. While individual sports like tennis and golf have many fans, they cannot compete with the popularity of team sports. The media foster near reverence for the stars, so inattentive reading of the sports pages might lead one to believe it is all about outstanding individual players. Obviously, stars play an important role, but winning coaches emphasize group cohesion over individual accomplishment because teamwork wins games and leads to championships. Winning teams mesh individuality and community; if players are too focused on their personal statistics, the team suffers. This is not meant to idealize team sports; cheating scandals and racism have tarnished many sports, but, at their best, they illustrate teamwork.

In addition, sports involve a social web wider than individual teams. Studs Terkel quotes a sports columnist who explained how interdependent we are: "'The players need one another, the fans need the players, the players need the fans, and the owners need both. It's all part of one community.'" However, he feared that that community had been lost: "'In the immediate future, I see as little chance for a sense of community in sports as I do for the larger world'" (Terkel 1998, 185). Sports can be a model of the importance of teamwork for all of life, but we often forget that in politics and the economy.

Teamwork played a large role in establishing and developing this nation. Many colonies, diverse as they were, worked together to form one nation. This is not to imply that the process was smooth; debates over a new constitution, for instance, were quite contentious, but those debates were about what was best for the public good, not for individual advantage.

Benefits of communities, in various forms (governmental, social, religious) have been and remain manifold. Yet the picture is not without blemishes; communities can also exclude. After Independence, immigrants from diverse lands, Irish, Italians, Eastern Europeans, Chinese, and others, came and helped build this nation. They were often victims of discrimination, to say nothing of forced emigration from Africa. Diversification has continued into the twenty-first century with some immigrants finding acceptance and others facing extreme discrimination. Blatant prejudice against descendants of people brought here as slaves, and non-WASPs in general, still exists. Many people refuse to recognize the significant contributions of these groups, all of them important members of Team USA. "We, the people" still does not include all the residents of this nation; we have forgotten "*e pluribus unum*."

We have gotten things backward; many seem to think government functions impede the individual. For example, some people think of taxes as theft, when they are really payments for valuable public services that benefit us all. As Nadia Urbinati puts it, "The language of the public good seems itself to have gone missing, the implication being that this same public good is a thing that penalizes individual merit rather than a condition for rewarding it" (Urbinati 2015, 7). We need not search very far to discover reasons for this disappearance.

Politicians and economists have undermined support for the public good. Ronald Reagan used class and racial divisiveness (remember the fiction about a Cadillac-driving welfare queen?) to win the presidency. He then rewarded the upper class with a significant tax cut while neglecting to remind the people of the myriad benefits taxes provide. Milton Friedman advocated maximizing shareholder value (at the cost of all the other stakeholders). Conservative Republicans, loyal servants of their masters, rewarded them with large tax cuts and significant benefits (e.g., government bailing out Wall Street but leaving Main Street to suffer from the Great Recession) while the working and middle classes got trivial tax reductions and minimal services. The cruelest cut, however, is that many in the middle class pay higher federal income taxes than billionaires. Both taxes and services are in sharp contrast to many European democracies. Public services that should be available to all are difficult to access and deficient because we have forgotten that we are all individuals within community.

Putnam writes that, in our history, the United States alternates between individualism and community; "except for a pause in the 1920s and early 1930s, Americans became steadily more connected socially from the 1890s to the 1960s, but then virtually all our measures show a steady, unrelenting decline in social connectedness over the last half century" (Putnam 2020, 162, see also 300; and Putnam, 2015, 206). He argues that this "Sixties pivot" has been very costly for the United States: "The indefensible economic inequality of the second Gilded Age, the political polarization that is enfeebling and endangering our democracy, the social fragmentation and isolation that ignore the basic human need for fellowship and most fundamentally, the self-centeredness that itself makes it so difficult to achieve the unity of purpose required to change our national course" (Putnam 2020, 313). And he notes that "researchers have steadily piled up evidence of how important social context, social institutions, and social networks—in short, our communities—remain for our well-being and our kids' opportunities" (Putnam 2015, 206).

Three major changes since the last quarter of the twentieth century, all with negative effect on the working and middle classes are noted by Robert Reich: "(1) the shift in corporate governance from stakeholder to shareholder capitalism, (2) the shift in bargaining power from large unions to giant corporations, and (3) the unleashing of the financial power of Wall Street" (Reich 2020, 95). He argues that these shifts have an "unfortunate and more lasting consequence" for the country: "an angry working class vulnerable to demagogues peddling authoritarianism, racism, and xenophobia" (Reich 2020, 122). The mayhem in Washington, DC, on January 6, 2021, is an example of what that can lead to.

Francis Fukuyama sees the United States as both individualistic and group-oriented but also notes that in recent decades "the balance has been shifting toward individualism rapidly" (Fukuyama 1995, 306). Fairness demands noting that this is not a new phenomenon; our history has alternated between more and less individualistic eras. Americans in the early Republic focused on their individual interests, not the public good, as John Adams recognized (see Chapter 4).

Individualism is obvious in the economy. While some businesspeople understand that profits depend on the interaction of multiple stakeholders, for instance that treating workers well is a profit maximizer, too many operate as individualist profit-seekers, regardless of the impact on workers, host communities, and the environment. Perhaps this is one reason that trust levels have been declining in our society (Edelman 2021).

Such decline is alarming because trust is imperative for capitalism and democracy; both are more effective when trust levels are high. The historic importance of trust is explained by Richard Layard:

> So if we trust each other, we have better possibilities open to us—the total take will be higher. The result of the cooperation is not zero sum; it is a win-win activity. If human beings had not been able to cooperate in this way, they would probably not have survived the rigours of the savannah—or subsequently of regions a lot colder. At best their life would have been, as Thomas Hobbes put

it, "solitary, poor, nasty, brutish and short." We survived because our genes gave us the ability to cooperate. (Layard 2005, 98)

Jesse Norman writes that in Adam Smith's *Wealth of Nations* markets "operate within a context of norms and trust which itself underwrites legal mechanisms of justice and enforcement" (Norman 2018, 162).

To function well, societies require trust; Virginia Held writes that "Perhaps what are needed for adequate levels of social cohesion are persons tied together by relations of concern and caring and empathy and trust rather than merely by contracts it may be in their interests to disregard" (Held, in Mansbridge 1990, 296). And she argues, "There are good reasons to believe that a society resting on no more than bargains between self-interested or mutually disinterested individuals will not be able to withstand the forces of egoism and dissolution pulling such societies apart" (Held, in Mansbridge 1990, 303). Similarly, Fukuyama argues that "reciprocity, moral obligation, duty toward community, and trust" are imperative for a modern society to succeed (Fukuyama 1995, 11).

Trust is also important for the economy. According to Joseph Stiglitz, events and economic research show "that no economy, not even a modern, market-based economy like America's, can function well without a modicum of trust—and that unmitigated selfishness inevitably diminishes trust" (Stiglitz 2015, 224). And he states, "Trust is what makes contracts, plans, and everyday transactions possible; it facilitates the democratic process, from voting to law creation, and is necessary for social stability. It is essential for our lives. It is trust, more than money, that makes the world go round" (Stiglitz 2015, 223). Emmanuel Saez and Gabriel Zucman concur, warning that "Relentless self-interest destroys the norms of trust and cooperation at the heart of any prosperous society" (Saez and Zucman 2019, viii).

Robert Nelson agrees on the importance of trust for the economy and makes a connection to religion: "The effective functioning of a market system requires a religious grounding to promote trust, inhibit opportunism, provide for implicit contracting, and serve in other ways to minimize transaction costs in society" (Nelson 2001, 301). Rupert Ederer notes Pope Benedict XVI's contention that a "social market" requires trust, quoting *Caritas in Veritate*: "*Without internal forms of solidarity and mutual trust, the market cannot completely fulfill its proper economic function*" (Ederer 2011, 197, italics in original).

What can be done to rebalance our society? The argument of this book is that the values of Adam Smith (Chapter 2), Christianity (Chapter 3), and John Adams (Chapter 4) suggest individuality within communities. Smith is called the "father of capitalism," but few people understand the sociable and ethical elements of his system. The individualism of many Christians ignores the Golden Rule. And Adams is included because his fears of the elite as a danger to democracy are applicable today. The founders were individuals but not individualists; they certainly differed in various ways, but Adams is included because of his warnings about a group (the aristocrats) who would undermine community.

INDIVIDUALITY WITHIN COMMUNITIES

John Adams and Adam Smith were strong advocates of liberty but not in the contemporary individualistic sense. No one can deny the individuality of these men. But the importance they attached to community makes it clear they did not advocate rugged individualism, which is so common today but was virtually unknown in their day.

Smith's system was a delicate balance of individuals and community. Anyone who reads *The Theory of Moral Sentiments*, which he considered to be his better book, will note the importance of community. That work's central concept, the impartial spectator, is incompatible with the extreme individualism from which we suffer today. *The Theory of Moral Sentiments* requires sociability, which we today might label empathy (a term not used until the twentieth century). His more famous and often misunderstood *Wealth of Nations* is an extended history of the growth and development of societies, from the earliest hunter-gatherers to eighteenth century Europe. In that work, the sociable community of *Theory* is assumed and the need for ethics in the economy is explicit. Moreover, his often-acerbic criticisms of businessmen could easily be used today as commentary on the excessive individualism of contemporary savage capitalism. These ideas are further developed in Chapter 2.

Christianity is based on individual salvation, but the individual act of conversion brings one into community; individualism was not known in ancient times. Community was so important in early Christianity that members held all goods in common—in other words, the Christian community was a proto-communist group (Acts 2:44–45 and 4:32–37). That degree of sharing does not characterize Christians today, but sociability is still essential to Christianity. This statement is based on the two great commandments, "love the Lord, your God," and "love your neighbor as yourself" (Matthew 22: 37–39), which, considered together, are clearly incompatible with individualism.

Researchers who examined multiple contemporary religious cooperative living communities in the United States wrote this: "Each member we talked to felt himself responsible to the Lord for their own life of faith, but also realized that the Christian life was meant to be a corporate life; that the Lord used individuals, but he used them best when they were bound together in faithful and loving harmony" (Jackson 2009, 23). The counterbalancing of individual and community is clear. Discussion of the individuals within community nature of Christianity is the subject of Chapter 3.

The founders were strong individuals from a variety of backgrounds, but they worked together to accomplish the improbable—independence from the mighty British empire. But, at the end of the Revolutionary War, John Adams feared the impact of factionalism, a smaller group profiting at the expense of the wider community. In a September 10, 1783, letter to William Gordon, Adams wrote: "In all domestick Disputes I wish our countrymen, may moderate their passions, & manifest as much mutual forbearance as possible. I dread the course of our elections if parties prevail" (Lint, XV 2010, 277). This is only one example of the many comments Adams made about the dangers of faction, which he feared would destroy democracy. The faction he feared most was the aristocracy (today we would say "the elites," a word not in common use until the nineteenth century). He hoped the new republic would be "a harmonious alliance of strong communities, not . . . [an] aggregation of self-centered individuals" (Ryerson 2016, 431). Adams and the founders wanted an inclusive political system but, instead, partisanship has prevailed; this is the subject of Chapter 4.

So, what does individuality within communities look like? Here are some examples of the contrast with individualism.

CONTRASTING INDIVIDUALISM AND INDIVIDUALITY WITHIN COMMUNITIES

Individualism	Individuality within Communities
Selfishness	Altruism
The star	The team
Either-or	Both-and/Yin-yang
Faction	Common good
Narcissism	Sociability
Intolerance	Tolerance
Religious dogmatism	Respect for other religions
Arrogance	Awareness of human fallibility
Polarization	Consensus
Ethnocentric, nationalistic	Universal
Exclusive (e.g., racism, sexism)	Inclusive
Go it alone	Social cohesion
Free rider	Mutuality
Every person for herself	The love ethic
Dictatorship/autocracy	Democracy
Patriarchy	Gender equality

Ownership	Stewardship of the earth
Maximize shareholder value	Maximize stakeholder value
Excessive executive compensation	Fair wages for all
Profit at any cost	Profit with integrity
Win at any cost	Play by the rules to win
Low taxes	Fair taxes
Militarism	Diplomacy
Special privilege	Equal justice

Source: Created by Author

Some readers may object that several examples in the individualism column involve multiple persons. They are listed in that column because they privilege a few at the expense of the many; they ignore the common good. But this work is not an argument for the dominance of communities to the exclusion of individuals; the individual is important as a member of multiple groupings. But individualism is criticized for its exclusion of others. Throughout this work, individualism is often used as shorthand for groups that focus on themselves to the exclusion of others, groups unconcerned about the common good.

Liberty is not just about individuals. We are social creatures and have lived in communities for millennia. We fought Great Britain for national liberty as a community of thirteen colonies. The individual colonies could not have gained liberty without unity; no individual colony could have succeeded alone. We value our independence, but that independence has always been within a context of interdependence. Today, international trade and climate change make interdependence obvious.

I am not arguing against specific individuals striving for their particular dreams; that is an important part of individuality. Each person is important, but she is not important in and of herself; she is important as a member of multiple communities. Nor am I arguing for submerging the individual in community; my both-and reasoning is about the dynamic interaction of opposites, not the dominance of either pole.

Individuality within communities might sound contradictory but many authors have appreciated the unity of opposites. For example, in *On Liberty,* published in 1859, John Stuart Mill repeatedly puts individuality into a societal context. While individual rights are, of course, central, the entire essay balances those rights in society. He wrote: "Whenever, in short, there is a definite damage, or a definite risk of damage, either to an individual or to the public, the case is taken out of the province of liberty, and placed in that of morality or law" (Mill 2011, 154). And "for such actions as are prejudicial to the interests of others, the individual is accountable and may be subjected either to social or to legal punishments, if society is of opinion that the one or the other is requisite for its protection" (Mill 2011, 177–78). In short, *On Liberty* balances individuality and sociability.

More recently, Judge Learned Hand, in a 1944 speech in Central Park, expressed this interaction.

> And what is this liberty which must lie in the hearts of men and women? It is not the ruthless, the unbridled will; it is not freedom to do as one likes. That is the denial of liberty, and leads straight to its overthrow. A society in which men recognize no check upon their freedom soon becomes a society where freedom is the possession of only a savage few; as we have learned to our sorrow.
>
> What then is the spirit of liberty? I cannot define it; I can only tell you my own faith. The spirit of liberty is the spirit which is not too sure that it is right; the spirit of liberty is the spirit which seeks to understand the mind of other men and women; the spirit of liberty is the spirit which weighs their interests alongside its own without bias. (Hand 1944)

He saw the sociable nature of individual freedom. But note also his openness to the truth held by others.

Martin Luther King Jr., analyzing society during the Cold War, wrote: "Communism fails to see the truth in individualism. Capitalism fails to realize that life is social. Communism fails to realize that life is personal. The good and just society is neither the thesis of capitalism nor the antithesis of Communism, but a socially conscious democracy which reconciles the truths of individualism and collectivism" (King 1967, 187).

Many authors argue that individuality and community need not be in conflict. Urbinati writes: "The relationship between liberty and equality is the thematic crux enabling us to understand and to evaluate the meaning of individualism in democratic society." (Urbinati 2015, 10–11). Free and equal individuals are necessary components of democratic communities. Putnam writes that it is simplistic to argue that there is "a zero-sum trade-off between communitarian equality and individualistic freedom"; and he states that we are a community of communities, a nation of communitarian virtues and individual liberties that must be balanced and integrated (Putnam 2020, 339–41). Fukuyama argues that the United States has a "dual heritage, both individualistic and group oriented" (Fukuyama 1995, 266, see also 272–73).

In other words, the individual is not eliminated by individuality within communities, as Cornel West explains:

> The norm of individuality reinforces the importance of community, common good, and the harmonious development of personality. And it stands in stark contrast to those doctrinaire individualisms which promote human selfishness, denigrate the idea of community, and distort the holistic development of

> personality. The norm of individuality conceives persons as enjoyers and agents of their uniquely human capacities, whereas doctrinaire individualism views them as maximizers of pleasure and appropriators of unlimited resources. (West 1982, 16–17).

He also refers to individuality "as self-realization within community" (West 1982, 123), a definition similar to Frances Lappe's "a person's individuality is constituted, not in defensive protection against society, but in that unique mix of relationships she or he bears to family, friends, neighbors, colleagues, and co-workers" (Lappe 1989,13).

This listing of dualistic thinkers demonstrates that the focus of this book is part of western thought; but, while the theme of this work is not compatible with the ideology of most economists, a few economists are both-and thinkers. Robert Nelson states, "The market requires a dual attitude with respect to self-interest—strong cultural inhibitions against the expression of self-interest (of opportunistic motives) in many areas of society; but at the same time strong encouragement for another powerful form of 'opportunism,' the individual pursuit of profit within the specific confines of the market" (Nelson 2001, 3, see also 9 and 268). That individual quest for self-advancement, a crucial part of a vibrant economy, should be constrained by community norms. The economist Herman Daly and theologian John Cobb, explain what that means: "instead of *homo economicus* as pure individual . . . *Homo economicus* [is] person-in-community" (Daly and Cobb 1989, 7).

The Christian social justice activist, A. J. Muste, using different words for the same concept, contrasts individuals with "persons anchored in historical communities and in God" (McCarraher 2000, 112). John Campbell and John Hall, sociologists, argue that markets work best when states can "*manage their economies effectively and when societies are blessed with basic social cohesion, so that the interests of the many in widespread prosperity are not outweighed by those of the privileged few*" (Campbell and Hall 2021, 1, italics in the original). And note what Anna Bernasek writes: "For too long, the economics profession has minimized the critical role of cooperation in economic activity. Emphasis on the individual has risen above all else and overshadowed the profound ways we depend on each other" (Bernasek 2010, 2). Jonathan Haidt's analysis of reciprocity experiments fits here as well (Haidt 2006).

Urbinati's grappling with the different meanings of individualism is also related: "Attention to the individual person and to her or his capacity to cooperate with others as equals in rights and dignity; attention to that individual person as a free and autonomous being whose judgment is at the source of the legitimacy of political authority: these are the political characteristics of democratic individualism" (Urbinati 2015, 5). In addition, she argues that we have divorced liberty from equality (in contrast to our Founders' declaration that all are created equal with an endowed right to liberty). This divorce turns "democratic individualism into an individualism that is antisocial and tyrannical, or apathetic and indifferent toward the fate of the wider human community, whether national or universal" (Urbinati 2015, 9).

Democratic individuality is concerned for others; mutuality is one way to describe such a community orientation. For instance, Sara Horowitz, discussing mutualism, writes this about unions, "The idea that workers did best when they formed institutions that allowed them to help themselves" (Horowitz 2021, 36). Russell Pregeant states the balance of individuality and community in mutuality: "To have genuine mutuality as one's goal is not to abandon the quest for individuated selfhood but to seek the development of a self that exists in relation to other selves" (Pregeant 2022, 142).

Paul Knowlton and Aaron Hedges also argue for mutuality, which they label "partnering," which "does not mean to prop others up with destructive selflessness (loving neighbor and not self), nor does it mean to push others down with destructive selfishness (loving self and not neighbor). Partnering is about mutual benefit . . . about keeping both the self and the other in view and acting profitably for both together" (Knowlton and Hedges 2021, 103; see also 87). They understand the complementary interrelationship of individuality and communities: "self-interest and common good reinforcing one another in a virtuous cycle of increasing value creation" (Knowlton and Hedges 2021, 131).

I read all these authors as thinking in yin-yang terms, "both-and," not "either-or"; individual and community are not mutually exclusive but are mutually reinforcing. Individuality in multiple communities strengthens people, but individualism is destructive. Each of us expresses our own individuality by the unique combination of communities to which we belong.

This is how we developed as a nation. Our Founders were individuals working for a more perfect union, an independent union of states that would promote both communities and individuality. As Barry Shain explains, independence did not mean individualism: "The only right besides that of religious conscience that Revolutionary-era Americans held to be inalienable, then, was the corporate right of a people to be self-governing" (Shain 1994, 256). Nancy Rosenblum writes, "From Tocqueville to Progressives at the turn of the twentieth century to participatory democrats and not a few conservative thinkers today, democracy is said to depend on 'the art and science of association'" (Rosenblum 2016, 214). Our democracy requires association, mutuality, partnership, not individualism.

There is an even more expansive definition of community that was the lodestar of Albert Schweitzer, an important twentieth-century humanist: reverence for life. He wrote, "The great fault of all ethics hitherto has been that they believed themselves to have to deal only with the relations of man to man. In reality, however, the question is what is his attitude to the world and all life that comes within his reach. A man is ethical only when life, as such, is sacred to him" (Schweitzer 1949, 126; see also 124 and 179). In this work, I will focus on individuality within human communities, but the reader will appreciate that the concept can be expanded to other living creatures. We are parts of an immense universe.

A skeptic might respond at this point that this is all very nice, but societies need individual productivity or people starve. Thomas Piketty rejects this approach: "The idea that each country (or worse yet, each person in each country) is individually responsible for its production and its wealth makes little sense from a historical point of view. All wealth is collective in origin" (Piketty 2022, 217). He adds that private property was initially designed to serve the common interest and put limits on individual wealth (Piketty 2022, 217).

The United States has been, although imperfectly, a land of opportunity, attracting immigrants from around the world. For generations, individuals and families, laboring on farms and in mines and factories, gradually advanced economically. While still attracting many immigrants and refugees, in recent decades the opportunities that made the quest for the American Dream realistic have been undermined by a new mercantilist class, a class that has used political clout to commandeer more and more of the economic benefits of American productivity as well as significant government benefits. It was similar mercantilism that Adam Smith analyzed and harshly criticized in *Wealth of Nations.*

Economic elites have successfully staged a stealth coup d'état. Our system should now be labeled plutocratic socialism for the wealthy with laissez-faire for the poor. Or as Reich puts it: "We already have socialism—for the very rich. Most Americans are subject to harsh capitalism" (Reich 2020, 8). This has meant, in the last half-century, steady increases in the income and wealth of billionaires while the middle and working classes suffer economically. And these changes in income distribution have had political impact, as Andres Solimano explains:

> The power of the financial elites is enormous, stemming from their capacity to manage resources and influence policymakers, regulators, and the central banks. They invest substantial money to make sure the monetary and financial authorities don't interfere with their operations and excursions, particularly during a boom phase of the financial cycle. Ironically, however, they require rescue packages when the boom stops. Their political power is one of the reasons austerity policies are imposed making the working and middle classes pay

> for their excesses. And yet the financial sector blames the welfare state for the crisis. (Solimano 2014, 109).

While there certainly were party disagreements in the post–World War II years, the more consensual politics of that era have been replaced by polarization. As Paul Krugman points out, "the Republican Party has moved right in tandem with the rising incomes of the elite, and political compromise has become almost impossible" (Krugman 2013, 88–9). If that sounds too bleak, many Americans still have a belief in democracy, and the United States has had waves of democratization (the Progressive Era, the New Deal). Perhaps we will awaken from our individualistic stupor and move toward democracy again. But for this to happen, inequalities in opportunity based on gender, race, and class, must be eliminated. A word of caution: this is not about the dictatorial propensities of any one person; we, as a society, need to pivot away from individualism, especially that extreme form labeled fascism.

The problem with pure individualism is exclusion, faction, liberty for a few at the expense of everyone else. Adam Smith, Christian leaders, and the Founders all emphasized inclusion, sociability, and justice. And sociability is a major factor contributing to happiness (a point developed in Chapter 6).

CONCLUSION

To recapitulate the main purpose, this work aims to show that sociability is a necessary component of Smith's market capitalism and is consistent with American religious and political values and traditions.

Greater sociability would revivify the perennial quest for democracy in the United States. Since the Declaration of Independence, this country has oscillated between more and less democratic governance. Since the 1970s, excessive individualism has transmuted our government into a plutocracy. Returning to a democratic trajectory is long overdue. For that to happen, it is imperative that individuality within communities replace individualism. Note the plural: "communities"; we are members of multiple communities. Singular community degenerates into conformity and thus is antithetical to individuality. Part of our individuality is that each of us participates in a variety of communities, our own unique set.

Next we examine the sociability of Adam Smith (the "Father of Capitalism"), and after that, Christianity and John Adams, all of which contrast to the excessive individualism of the United States in the twenty-first century. These chapters are followed by chapters on benefits from community, arguing that markets are much more community dependent than laissez-faire advocates admit and that greater sociability improves happiness.

Chapter Two

Adam Smith's Sociability

Individualism and capitalism are the Siamese twins of the US market economy. But Adam Smith did not advocate individualistic capitalism, which some analysts call free-market fundamentalism. Three misunderstandings of Smith's writings have resulted in an excessively individualistic market system. Many think laissez-faire is part of his capitalism, but he never used the term. The impartial spectator, an important component of his systematic analysis, is ignored. And the invisible hand is assigned a large role in the market, even though he rarely used it in his large body of works. All three reinforce individualistic freedom, thereby undermining the sociability of the impartial spectator. Let us examine these misunderstandings.

Smith's market economy does not include laissez-faire, a term that is antithetical to the sociable market with equal opportunity and justice that he actually advocated. Obviously, liberty is an important aspect of a democratic market economy, but Smith completely disagreed with laissez-faire. He did not use the term, even though he was very familiar with the concept. He did not write about absolute liberty (a connotation of laissez-faire) but about a society constrained by the impartial spectator and, if necessary, government.

More than two centuries of emphasis on laissez-faire has grossly distorted capitalism; liberty has been emphasized while equality and justice have been excluded. When these are included, markets are sociable, not individualistic. As Oreskes and Conway put it, "There are many capitalisms. American market fundamentalists fight for a form of capitalism that is both brutal and ignorant; that rushes aside market failure, anticompetitive practices, and external costs, in part by denying the facts of science, the facts of history, and the necessary role of government in making capitalism work" (Oreskes and Conway 2023, 390–91). "Free market" advocates ignore the sociability, equality, and justice that were fundamental in Smith's system.

His extensive body of published and unpublished works was intended as analysis of all knowledge. Such an enormous research and writing project was not unreasonable for Smith, a polymath. Unfortunately, he was also a meticulous writer, revising his work multiple times so he never finished his grand plan. But we do know that it was all part of a comprehensive view of the world. Writing about *Theory of Moral Sentiments* and *Wealth of Nations,* Robert Heilbroner notes that "the dovetailing of the two works illustrates the remarkable unity of Smith's larger conception of the human universe, a unity that pervades all his works from the lectures on rhetoric and the essay on Astronomy to his inquiry into Political Economy" (Heilbroner 1982, 435). More recently, a British scholar, writing about a 1761 Smith essay on languages, emphasizes "the interconnectedness of his thought from the very start of his intellectual journey" (Norman 2018, 37). Thus, what he wrote in various essays and in *Theory of Moral Sentiments,* his first book, is important for interpreting his other book, the more famous *Wealth of Nations.*

Smith's approach was a nuanced one of individuals enmeshed in multiple social relationships. His emphasis on human sociability is crystal clear in the first sentence of *Theory.* "How selfish soever man may be supposed, there are evidently some principles in his nature, which interest him in the fortune of others, and render their happiness necessary to him, though he derives nothing from it except the pleasure of seeing it" (Smith 1790, I 1–2). Given his emphasis on sociability in *Theory,* "he derives nothing from it" seems like an understatement. One might not gain anything concrete from sociability; but "the pleasure of seeing it" indicates a contribution to happiness.

Commenting on this sentence, Ryan Hanley writes that Smith sees humans as neither egocentric nor altruistic. "Smith regards our natural condition as one of division, and specifically one divided between concerns for others and concerns for ourselves" (Hanley 2016, 126). But this division is not a psychological pathology; the reality of human existence is that we are all individuals within multiple communities. Norman, contrasting modern ideas of individualism with Smith's ideas, states that he did not see "people as individual atoms at all . . . within his system, individuals cannot be given independent definition; they are seen as continuously dynamically defined and redefined through their relations with others" (Norman 2018, 200).

This is a fine balancing act; dominance by either individualism or community produces pathology, ranging from narcissism on the one hand to totalitarianism on the other.

Smith's "both-and" mode of thinking, which pervades his entire body of work, is widely understood by scholars. For instance, Warren Samuels writes that Smith "did comprehend great truths whose wisdom and accuracy resided in their synthesis with opposites which were also true in distinguishable respects." But "ideological filtration" has "distorted and emasculated Smith's analysis" (Samuels 1977, 195). Perhaps the greatest distortion has been the emphasis that market fundamentalists place on laissez-faire, a free market system, an approach Smith did not advocate.

LAISSEZ-FAIRE

In *Wealth of Nations,* Smith advocated ethical market capitalism. He understood that if businessmen were not ethical, the government would have to intervene to provide fairness in the market. In *Wealth,* he suggested a long list of government interventions (see Hill 2016, 21–60). But Smith's ideal social order is not the prevailing model of capitalism today. Both in the United States and Europe, economists and other interpreters of Smith emphasize free markets, arguing that he advocated laissez-faire. Note that this misinterpretation was so pervasive that, late in the nineteenth century, the president of the Massachusetts Institute of Technology (MIT) stated that belief in laissez-faire was a prerequisite for being an economist (Prindle 2006, 104). That belief, and its corollary belief in individualism, has been even stronger in the twentieth and twenty-first centuries.

According to Andy Denis, throughout the twentieth century, "the standard view of Adam Smith among economists" was "a simple and straightforward individualism" (Denis 1999, 71–2). Smith's sociable, ethical, and egalitarian liberty was replaced with a no-holds-barred free market, which produced enormous inequality in the richest nation in the world. Ironically, this means liberty is real only for those who can afford it. It includes enormous government benefits for the wealthy; because the tax code is written to minimize their taxes, enabling some millionaires to have no income tax liability. These benefits come with little or no cost to the plutocrats but enormous cost to society, with many people highly constrained by poverty, debt, and insufficient government services. Smith actually advocated both liberty and greater sociability; his thought is in stark contrast to the individualistic license of our contemporary market.

We have been living in a dream world of free market individualism. Books such as Ayn Rand's *Atlas Shrugged* and Milton Friedman's *Free to Choose* both reflected and reinforced that idea; they attracted many with a dream that the United States could be different from the rest of the world by having an individualistic, laissez-faire economic system. Reich calls market fundamentalism "a religion that idolizes the free market while masking those with power over the rules of the game" (Reich 2020, 189). This secular religion was based on an important partial truth: markets are immensely powerful ways to organize economic relationships.

Many politicians took up the Rand/Friedman cry. Years of repetition of their ideas (regulations only make things worse, government is the problem) convinced many people that any government involvement in the economy was a socialist violation of laissez-faire. One result was that regulations were relaxed or abandoned with catastrophic impact on the middle and working classes. Capitalism has become a game in which weak regulation allows insiders to reap enormous rewards; it is not Smith's capitalism.

The ideologues' dream world is a nightmare for most people. Free market absolutists took an important truth, the efficacy of market systems, and reduced it to the absurd. The freedom of a nation of small shopkeepers (freedom within ethical constraints) does not work with modern corporate behemoths. Modern corporations have destroyed market capitalism because no individual can stand up to them. Markets have been replaced by insider games. Governments must intervene to restore a functioning fair market because, for most citizens, laissez-faire is anything but fair.

Smith was intimately familiar with laissez-faire, because of his 1764–1766 tour of France as tutor of the Duke of Buccleugh. While on that trip, he started to write a book, probably *Wealth of Nations*. In a letter to Hume from Toulouse, dated July 5, 1764, noting that he had little to do, he wrote, "I have begun to write a book to pass away the time" (Mossner 1987, 102).

On that tour, he met the Physiocrats and had significant discussions with them. Zoltan Haraszti quotes a Physiocrat who wrote about conversations with Smith: "'We discussed the theory of commerce, banking, public credit, and many points of his great work, the *Wealth of Nations*, which he was meditating'" (Haraszti 1952, 328). Smith respected them and had more than ample time to integrate their idea of laissez-faire into his system. *Wealth of Nations* was published in 1776, a decade after his return from France, but he did not use their term. Given the particular care with which he wrote, the exclusion is quite significant. The logical deduction is that he disagreed with the concept.

How can one be so certain? After all, Smith died more than two centuries ago. Laissez-faire advocates argue that he abandoned the sociability of *Theory* for individualism in *Wealth*; their argument relies on an assumption that he changed his mind between writing his first and second books. The argument is illogical on several counts.

Emphasizing laissez-faire ignores the cohesion of Smith's works. He was a rigorously logical and systematic thinker, according to multiple Smith scholars. His first biographer and literary executor, Dugald Stewart, wrote of this "love of system" (Smith 1982, 306; see also 323). His never-completed grand project was designed to synthesize all knowledge into one integrated whole; he was theorizing about the entire world throughout history. As Samuels states, "Interpretation cannot properly reduce Smith's analysis to single-factor explanations or to narrow normative systems without doing injury to his synoptic and synthetic view of the realities of economic life" (Samuels 1977, 194).

Smith saw his work as scientific, modeled on the work of Isaac Newton (Prindle 2006, 9). But note that, according to Lisa Hill, he was "not scientific in the purely descriptive, 'hard science' sense but in the sense particular to eighteenth-century usage, namely, as a 'body of systematic knowledge' with normative implications for what, practically, ought to be done, in this case, by legislators" (Lisa Hill, in Hanley 2016, 326). It should always be remembered that Smith made his reputation as a moral philosopher; *Wealth of Nations* was the extension of his moral-ethical system to the socio-political realm, not abandonment of that system.

As a systematic thinker, Smith did not abandon the sociability for *Theory* to individualism in *Wealth.* This is clear from Stewart's comment that, for Smith, every government should "make as equitable a distribution as possible, among all the different members of a community, of the advantages arising from the political union" (Smith 1982, 309–10). Let me emphasize: "all the members," not a few fortunate individualists. Smith's systematic thinking is also understood by other scholars (Skinner 1996, 2; Heilbroner 1982, 435; Minowitz 1993, 6).

His corpus of works was consistent in emphasizing sociability, precisely what one would expect of a systematic thinker. Patricia Werhane argues that sociability, cooperation, is important in *Wealth* as well as in *Theory* (Werhane 1991, 11). He did not reject sociability when he published *Wealth* seventeen years after *Theory.* Hanley notes that Smith's 1790 revision of *Theory* added a new section on the importance of morality for natural liberty (Hanley 2009, 86). D. D. Raphael and A. L. Macfie, editors of an Oxford University Press edition of *Theory* clearly state that his works are linked: "Essentially, however, TMS and WN are at one" (Smith, 1976, *9*). Moreover, they state that Smith clearly regarded *Wealth* "as continuing the sequence of thought set out in TMS . . . the new material in edition 6 [of TMS] is simply a development of Smith's earlier position and at the same time reflects some of the interests of WN" (Smith, 1976, 24).

For markets to be just, they need moral interactions; Smith's moral system was explicitly sociable (Hill 2016, 31–5). Justice is an important part of Smith's market economy as presented in *Wealth of Nations,* and it was a major concept in *Theory,* as Stewart points out (Stewart, in Smith 1982, 285).

Smith was well aware of the dangers of being a "man of system," but he saw his work as scientific (in the social science, not natural science sense) (Smith 1790, II 110; Ross 1995, 355). He had a comprehensive plan of research and writing, which was never completed (possibly because he was such a perfectionist, continually revising his two published works). He did not abandon the sociability of *Theory* when he wrote *Wealth of Nations*, and he did not endorse laissez-faire.

To grasp Smith's complex thought fully, one must understand his impartial spectator.

THE IMPARTIAL SPECTATOR

That sociability permeates *Theory of Moral Sentiments* is perhaps nowhere clearer than in his description of the impartial spectator. We learn appropriate behavior by imagining how our actions would appear through the eyes of other people.

> We either approve or disapprove of our own conduct, according as we feel that, when we place ourselves in the situation of another man, and view it, as it were, with his eyes and from his station, we either can or cannot entirely enter into and sympathize with the sentiments and motives which influenced It. . . . We endeavor to examine our own conduct as we imagine any other fair and impartial spectator would examine it. If, upon placing ourselves in his situation, we thoroughly enter into all the passions and motives which influenced it, we approve of it, by sympathy with the approbation of this supposed equitable judge. (Smith 1790, I 276–77).

Reading this, one might wonder why Smith did not use the word "empathy." He did not have that option because that word was not used until a century after he wrote. It seems clear that basing one's behavior on the impartial spectator requires empathy. One must go outside oneself and apply a sense of whether behavior is acceptable to community to determine how one lives. This requires one to live interdependently, in harmony with others. Norman writes that such harmony "of humans is the hinge of Smith's entire system" (Norman 2018, 58). Note "entire system"; sociability applies to *Wealth of Nations*, as well.

An intricate interplay of self-love and sensitivity to the expectations of society is obvious when Smith contrasts our powerful selfish feelings and "a stronger power," our "generous and noble" active principles:

> It is reason, principle, conscience, the inhabitant of the breast, the man within, the great judge and arbiter of our conduct. It is he who, whenever we are about to act so as to affect the happiness of others, calls to us, with a voice capable of astonishing the most presumptuous of our passions, that we are but one of the multitude, in no respect better than any other in it; and that when we prefer ourselves so shamefully and so blindly to others, we become the proper objects of resentment, abhorrence, and execration. It is from him only that we learn the real littleness of ourselves, and of whatever relates to ourselves, and the natural misrepresentations of self-love can be corrected only by the eye of this impartial spectator. It is he who shows us the propriety of generosity and the deformity of injustice; the propriety of resigning the greatest interests of our own for the yet greater interests of others, and the deformity of doing the smallest injury

> to another, in order to obtain the greatest benefit to ourselves. (Smith 1790, I 336–37).

Self-interest was not to be pursued at the expense of other individuals within the community.

Smith traces this line of reasoning back to "all the ancient sects of philosophers" but especially the Stoics, who, he writes, argued that man "ought to regard himself, not as something separated and detached, but as a citizen of the world, a member of the vast commonwealth of nature. To the interest of this great community, he ought at all times to be willing that his own little interest should be sacrificed" (Smith 1790, I 344–45). Adam Smith's sociable impartial spectator is completely antithetical to individualism.

He also connects the impartial spectator to the Christian commandment to love one's neighbor as one loves oneself. And in the same paragraph he writes "that to feel much for others and little for ourselves, that to restrain our selfish, and to indulge our benevolent affections, constitutes the perfection of human nature" (Smith 1790, I 47). He also argues that "human happiness arises from the consciousness of being beloved" (Smith 1790, I 96). Human beings want to be loved and praised, not hated and blamed (Smith 1790, I 284–85; see also 292–93, and 415–16).

This desire to be loved reinforces a willingness to sacrifice individual interest for the greater good: "The wise and virtuous man is at all times willing that his own private interest should be sacrificed to the public interest of his own particular order or society . . . the interest of this order or society should be sacrificed to the greater interest of the state . . . all those inferior interests should be sacrificed to the greater interest of the universe" (Smith 1790, II 115). Note the inclusive dimensions of Smith's sociability: not merely a matter of family or community, it encompasses all of creation.

Smith attributes the virtues of prudence, justice, and "proper beneficence" to the impartial spectator. That arbiter reproaches us for too little or too much frugality or industry, and for "our inattention to our own happiness, and for our still greater indifference and inattention, perhaps, to that of other people" (Smith 1790, II 187–88). Individual interests and the interests of others are both important; neither should be neglected.

Concern for others does not mean that Smith misunderstood the human propensity for self-interested behavior. Perhaps the best way to explain Smith's thinking is individuality within communities, sociability, not individualism. Excessive self-interest was not acceptable.

> There can be no proper motive for hurting our neighbour, there can be no incitement to do evil to another, which mankind will go along with, except just indignation for evil which that other has done to us. To disturb his happiness merely

> because it stands in the way of our own, to take from him what is of real use to him merely because it may be of equal or of more use to us, or to indulge, in this manner, at the expence of other people, the natural preference which every man has for his own happiness above that of other people, is what no impartial spectator can go along with. (Smith 1790, I 204–5).

Contemporary scholars understand that the individualism of the pure self-interest model does not explain all economics, in particular, "questions about labor market interactions, public goods, and social norms," according to Ernst Fehr and Simon Gächter. They argue that progress in these areas requires analysis of reciprocity (Fehr and Gächter 2000, 22). Haidt, a psychologist, argues that by using reciprocity, "we create an ultrasocial world, a world in which we refrain from nearly all the ways we could take advantage of those weaker than us, a world in which we often help those who are unlikely ever to be able to return the favor. We *want* to play tit for tat, which means starting out nice without being a pushover, and we *want* to cultivate a reputation for being a good player. Gossip and reputation make sure that what goes around comes around." (Haidt 2006, 55).

In short, a capitalist market economy does not require individualism and is incompatible with Smith's empathetic, sociable impartial spectator. Such sociability is in stark contrast to the individualistic liberty of so many people today.

Words shift their meanings over time. The dominant interpretation of liberty has changed since the eighteenth century; today many assume its meaning is laissez-faire individualism, ignoring Smith's sociable liberty. They incorrectly trace that interpretation back to *Wealth of Nations,* but what he advocated was a sociable market, not a free market.

SOCIABILITY

Smith argued that people require society in order to exist. "All the members of human society stand in need of each other's assistance, and are likewise exposed to mutual injuries." But beyond mere existence, society is imperative for a higher quality of life. "Where the necessary assistance is reciprocally afforded from love, from gratitude, from friendship, and esteem, the society flourishes and is happy. All the different members of it are bound together by the agreeable bands of love and affection, and are, as it were, drawn to one common centre of mutual good offices" (Smith 1790, I 213).

That humans are sociable is fundamental to *Theory of Moral Sentiments*, but it is also important in *Wealth of Nations.* Heilbroner notes that one theme of *Theory,* important for integration with *Wealth*, is the transformation of humans "into socialized man, the actor who inhabits and activates the moral and economic world with which Smith is concerned" (Heilbroner 1982, 429). The market is not without guardrails; it is bounded by the impartial spectator.

In *Wealth*, Smith clearly states that the quest for economic advancement cannot be individualistic. He writes about the cooperative nature of markets; the poorest person in a civilized country could not be provided with his minimal provisions "without the assistance and co-operation of many thousands" (Smith 1791, I 19). He follows this comment with the usually misconstrued discussion of the self-interest of the butcher and the baker (Smith 1791, I 21–22). The butcher's and the baker's self-interest gets them nowhere without connecting to the self-interest of others. They have to be cooperative, aware of their customers' needs, if they want to maximize profit. If they do not compete on quality, service, and price—if they do not provide what the customers want—they go bankrupt. The butcher cannot be an anomic individualist; to be successful, self-interest rightly understood is needed. One has to cooperate with others to have a thriving business, even if one is selling the necessities of life.

The argument for sociability does not depend solely on *Theory of Moral Sentiments*. *Wealth of Nations* assumes a sociable market context. According to John Kay, "Markets function well only when embedded in strong and supportive social institutions" (Kay 2018, 5). Kay also writes that Smith understood "that a successful market economy requires the legal, social and economic infrastructure that only a strong state can provide. . . . There is no contradiction between *Moral Sentiments* and *Wealth*" (Kay 2018, 5). Kay's conclusion is no surprise, given the systematic nature of Smith's writing.

While patriotism (the "last refuge of a scoundrel") can be individualistic, it can also be a clear example of sociability.

> The love of our country seems, in ordinary cases, to involve in it two different principles; first, a certain respect and reverence for that constitution or form of government which is actually established; and secondly, an earnest desire to render the condition of our fellow-citizens as safe, respectable, and happy as we can. He is not a citizen who is not disposed to respect the laws and to obey the civil magistrate; and he is certainly not a good citizen who does not wish to promote, by every means in his power, the welfare of the whole society of his fellow-citizens. (Smith 1790, II 104).

Such concern for others contrasts with rugged individualism. As an example, he cited "good soldiers" for their willingness to die for their country: "They cheerfully sacrifice their own little systems to the prosperity of a greater system" (Smith 1790, II 116). An individualist would see that statement as absolute nonsense, but as Robert Frank points out, such sacrifice is not unusual for

Congressional Medal of Honor winners. He notes that "our highest military honor has often been awarded posthumously to soldiers who threw themselves atop live grenades to save their comrades. Surely not even the most dedicated rationalist would pretend that these soldiers somehow figured to come out ahead" (Frank 1988, 213).

Patriotism, for Smith, did not mean love for one's country to the exclusion of the rest of the world. For instance, his better-known book is entitled *Wealth of Nations,* not *Wealth of Great Britain.* Giovanni Arrighi argues that Smith advocated a "commonwealth of civilizations," including all the nations of the world (Arrighi 2007, 9–10). Smith loved his country while criticizing its policies, with the goal of promoting more effective ones. More effective policies for increasing wealth meant that Britain should participate in an interdependent world, as *Wealth of Nations* clearly argued.

Sociability is not just about patriotism; Frank states that selfless behavior occurs in many other situations, in ways that are inconsistent "with the classical portrait of economic man" (Frank 1988, 213; see also ix). He also argues that the self-interest model that has dominated the field of economics is "a woefully inadequate description of the way people actually behave" (Frank 1988, 256). Reciprocal altruism (a form of sociability) is more common than the self-interest model predicts (Frank 1988, 221).

Other authors also emphasize Smith's sociability. Remy Debes, for example, notes that Smith was one of several eighteenth-century thinkers, including Hutcheson and Hume, critical of "early modern forms of egoism, and in particular Mandeville's then notorious *Fable of the Bees*" (Debes, in Hanley 2016, 192). Smith understood self-interest as a synonym for selfishness; he would not have comprehended twenty-first-century individualism. Michael Biziaou states that individualism was a category unknown to Smith (Biziaou, in Hanley 2016, 426–27). Samuel Fleischacker writes that Smith is "aligned with those who argued *against*" writers such as Hobbes and Mandeville, well known for their self-interest writings (Fleischacker 2002, 917–18).

For years, scholars have argued that Smith, in contrast to Mandeville, was not "an apostle of selfishness" (Hanley 2016, ix). Peter Whybrow notes that "In Smith's optimistic vision, in a market-based economy, greed and similarly undesirable behaviors of the self would be held in check by the powerful human need for love and neighborly social acceptance, resulting in the provision of 'universal opulence' for all" (Whybrow 2004, 57). His sociability is clearly explained by Norman who wrote that Smith's community orientation generates socio-moral norms of "awareness of others, courtesy, open-mindedness, consideration, tolerance and respect" (Norman 2018, 303).

Modern individualists seem unaware of Smith's emphasis on sociability, which Peter Minowitz describes: Smith's "relationship of human individuals to one another is thus characterized by a blend of separateness and unity. We distinguish mine and thine; we need 'cooperation and assistance'" (Minowitz 1993, 72).

According to Vivienne Brown, "The sociality of human life is fundamental for Adam Smith's writings . . . any inquiry into ways of life, history, or morals must start from an understanding of this sociality rather than from any notion of an individual abstracted from social context" (Brown, in Hanley 2016, 17). Note Brown's "Adam Smith's writings": she is not referring only to *Theory of Moral Sentiments.* He did not replace the social emphasis of *Theory* with profit-maximizing individualism when he wrote *Wealth of Nations.* Remember, he was working on a grand system. Jerry Evensky also states the importance of sociability in *Wealth of Nations*: "An oft-neglected thread that weaves its way through his analysis of the progressive development of the wealth of nations is that such progress is impossible without simultaneous, appropriate development of social and political institutions" (Evensky, in Hanley 2016, 67). These social and political institutions were intended to benefit everyone. Absolute liberty was not a part of his ideal social order; liberty was, instead, constrained by justice and equal opportunity.

Smith was not alone in limiting individual liberty. The boundary of liberty is an issue that thinkers have long debated. For instance, almost a century after the founding of this nation, in *On Liberty,* John Stuart Mill argued that "where to place the limit—how to make the fitting adjustment between individual independence and social control—is a subject on which nearly everything remains to be done" (Mill 2011, 9). I contend that the issue is still unresolved and hope that this work contributes to the discussion. Too much social control destroys liberty, but unbounded liberty threatens democracy and equal opportunity.

And the sociable Smith was inclusive in his compassion.

THE COMPASSIONATE SMITH

He believed a market economy could promote the well-being of all socio-economic classes: "Smith's ultimate quest was social justice. He advocated an open market with economic and social protocols between countries that would result in an overall improvement in the living conditions of the common citizen" (Ward 2007, 45–6).

His compassion was not restricted to one race or class. In *Theory of Moral Sentiments,* he wrote:

> There is not a negro from the coast of Africa who does not, in this respect, possess a degree of magnanimity which the soul of his sordid master is too often scarce capable of conceiving. Fortune never exerted more cruelly her empire

over mankind, than when she subjected those nations of heroes to the refuse of the jails of Europe, to wretches who possess the virtues neither of the countries which they come from, nor of those which they go to, and whose levity, brutality, and baseness, so justly expose them to the contempt of the vanquished. (Smith 1790, II 37)

Sensitivity to different races is also clear in a section of *Wealth of Nations* dealing with the discovery of the Americas and of the Cape of Good Hope route to Asia. He saw these discoveries as generally beneficial but also noted a negative impact on indigenous peoples: "To the natives, however, both of the East and West Indies, all the commercial benefits which can have resulted from those events have been sunk and lost in the dreadful misfortunes which they have occasioned" (Smith 1791, II 458-–59).

Amartya Sen emphasizes this racial egalitarianism: "Adam Smith's stubborn opposition to the racism, imperial prejudice, ethnic snobbery and intellectual arrogance common among influential people in the world around him, indicates how far ahead of his time Smith was as a morally sensitive thinker" (Sen, in Hanley 2016, 301; see also 299).

Smith foresaw that, over time, the colonies might grow stronger, leading to respect among nations: "But nothing seems more likely to establish this equality of force than that mutual communication of knowledge and of all sorts of improvements which an extensive commerce from all countries to all countries naturally, or rather necessarily, carries along with it" (Smith 1791, II 459). His advocacy of free trade is, of course, common knowledge.

He made similarly egalitarian comments about socio-economic class:

> The difference between the most dissimilar characters, between a philosopher and a common street porter, for example, seems to arise not so much from nature, as from habit, custom, and education. When they came into the world, and for the first six or eight years of their existence, they were, perhaps, very much alike and neither their parents nor playfellows could perceive any remarkable difference. (Smith 1791, I 23–4).

He thought the various classes and races of people were fundamentally the same. And he wrote that new industrial techniques could promote equality. The division of labor made it possible for all classes to be wealthy: "It is the great multiplication of the production of all the different arts, in consequence of the division of labour, which occasions, in a well-governed society, that universal opulence which extends itself to the lowest ranks of the people" (Smith 1791, I 16). And, in Book IV of *Wealth,* he included a similar statement: "The establishment of perfect justice, of perfect liberty, and of perfect equality, is the very simple secret which most effectually secures the highest degree of prosperity to all the three classes" (Smith 1791, IV 13). It should be noted that he did not list "liberty" first. He wrote about a market economy that combined ethical business practices with equal opportunity, which would result in widespread wealth.

Note the insistence on a "well-governed society." The enormous economic gap between the billionaire class and most Americans, but especially the poor, demonstrates that the United States is not well governed. The common assumption that a free market is best is not compatible with Smith's sociable concern for all the classes.

Perhaps it is such comments that led Fleischacker to argue that "people might have a right not to be poor." He also argues that Smith saw the poor and the wealthy as equal human beings; in comparison to the wealthy, the average poor person was "equal in intelligence, virtue, ambition, and interests with every other human being, hence equal in rights and desert, in dignity" (Fleischacker, in Hanley 2016, 485–86).

In his empathy for the poor, Smith differed significantly from contemporary American individualists. His advocacy of education for the common man, for instance, shows this concern, as Lisa Hill explains:

> It is significant that the indicators Smith used to test how well states were governed did not include traditional markers like extent of conquered territory or the amount of stockpiled gold but referred to factors that directly affected the lives of the average person: available food supply, population levels, productivity and employment levels, general living conditions, education standards, and mortality rates. He was concerned with welfare and positive outcomes for the population in general. (Lisa Hill, in Hanley 2016, 325).

Smith did not condone dissipation among the poor, but he also did not see the poor, in general, as dissipated. Social policies in many European countries today seem consistent with his sympathetic understanding of poverty.

He was a bit Calvinistic in his attitudes to luxury; wealth should be reinvested in productive facilities instead of being wasted on gold and silver which he called "trifling superfluities" (Smith 1791, I 374–75). But he also wrote approvingly about the lower classes emulating the wealthy. If an individual, through hard work and creativity (and probably some good luck) made it big, that person appeared to the lower classes to have everything. When that success was attained ethically, that individual was a model for the lower classes to emulate. Smith thought that the emulation function was good for motivation. But how one obtained wealth mattered; remember, his simple recipe for wealth was justice, liberty, and equality. He wanted people to emulate the ethical rich, not greedy individualists. In other words, people should not emulate the robber barons, the Bernie Madoffs, the Michael Milkins.

In his egalitarianism, Smith was consistent with other Enlightenment writers, who, according to Jonathan Wight, "rejected the elitist notion that either a hierarchical or hereditary authority was necessary to promote the political, economic, or moral order. They believed that all humans were created equal, and it was experience and opportunity, not difference in ability, that distinguished the king or philosopher from the average man" (Wight 2007, 344). It should be easy for Americans to understand this, given the "all men are created equal" language of the Declaration of Independence.

This interpretation of Smith's sociability is not only a liberal perspective; some economic conservatives recognize that his system included an important social dimension. For instance, Paul Heyne writes that Smith did not see man as selfish (Heyne 2008, 58). Heyne is also aware of Smith's "both-and" thinking; the individual is important, but so is society: "The units of analysis in Adam Smith's social vision are individuals; but the object of understanding is the cooperation that occurs among them. Self-love is assumed; but so is respect for the laws of justice" (Heyne 2008, 95–6). In this context, it must be noted that, for Smith, the "laws of justice" were both governmental and ethical.

It should be obvious that this is not an argument that liberty is unimportant; it clearly plays a large role in any market economy. But Smith's use of "natural liberty" has been distorted by advocates of individualism as support for their expanded conception of the meaning of liberty. Shain notes that eighteenth-century Americans' sense of liberty "offered only a narrow range of permissible behavior" (Shain 1994, 161). Much of what we see today as liberty would have been seen as license by that generation. "This fundamentally medieval and early modern corporate sense of liberty has disappeared from contemporary usage" (Shain 1994, 162). And Shain is critical of a continued "willingness of students of politics to ascribe anachronistic meaning to important 18th Century moral and political terms" (Shain 1994, 158–59; see 169–81 *et passim* for his discussion of eight different meanings of liberty in the eighteenth century, only one of which was modern individualistic freedom). His "corporate sense of liberty" could be called individuality within communities.

Emphasis on individual liberty also requires "proof texting," citing specific texts while ignoring the systematic nature of Smith's writing. For instance, this sentence in *Wealth of Nations* is easy to proof text: "the obvious and simple system of natural liberty establishes itself of its own accord." But in the same paragraph, Smith goes on to list three major areas for government action: international defense, "an exact administration of justice," and public works (Smith 1791, III 42–3). All three functions are inherently sociable.

In the past, citizens shared the burden of defending the nation. While there were always a few individuals who used bone spurs and similar medical excuses for avoiding military service, most people responded patriotically when drafted; large numbers volunteered for World War I and World War II. But with the advent of the all-volunteer military, enlistment has become more individualistic.

The second and third government roles have been impeded by excessive individualism. Considering the administration of justice first, it is important to remember Smith's belief that *Theory,* with its emphasis on justice, was his better work. Note that justice, for Smith, was both juridical (governmental) and moral/ethical. Ethics and morality were also heavily emphasized in *Wealth* (see Hill 2016, 31–46 for detailed support for this statement). At least one conservative thinker, Heyne, understands the importance of justice in Smith's thinking: "Legislation is unjust, in Smith's view, when it promotes the interests of one group of citizens by imposing unequal restraints on the actions of other groups. . . . The Smithian system is fundamentally misunderstood by anyone who ignores the role Smith assigns to 'the laws of justice' in shaping legislation and restraining self-interested behavior" (Heyne 2008, 87–8). When capitalism becomes a game in which insiders reap enormous rewards because of lack of transparency and lack of regulation, it is no longer Smith's capitalism. Who can stand up to such greed? Only a strong government, willing to advocate for a market with justice.

The extreme individualistic interpretation of Smith is also incompatible with his extensive list of public works in *Wealth* (see Kennedy 2010, 122–23, and Hill 2016, 47–9). Public works have long suffered from inadequate funding in the United States. Individualistic anti-tax rhetoric, designed to "starve the beast," has instead contributed to obscenely inflated federal debt (mortgaging the future of generations yet unborn) and has impoverished crucial government services. This results in collapsing bridges and inefficient, overcrowded public transit systems, only two examples of underfunding the common good. This approach is explicitly contrary to Smith's ideal society: man "is sensible too that his own interest is connected with the prosperity of society, and that the happiness, perhaps the preservation of his existence, depends upon its preservation" (Smith 1790, I 219–20).

That he did not see natural liberty as absolute is also clear in his comments about the importance of education for working class children: "The publick can impose upon almost the whole body of the people the necessity of acquiring those most essential parts of education, by obliging every man to undergo an examination or probation in them before he can obtain the freedom in any corporation, or be allowed to set up any trade either in a village or town corporate" (Smith 1791, III 188). This is in sharp contrast with his arguments in *Wealth* against restrictions on the liberty of tradesmen (Smith 1791, I 151 and 188); but education was so important to Smith that he was willing to restrict going into business as a tradesman, if one could not demonstrate the education needed to fulfill roles as parent, worker, citizen, and soldier.

Smith recognized that it is difficult for people to view their own behavior "in the light in which any indifferent spectator would consider it" (Smith 1790, I 292–93). In the twenty-first century, such self-evaluation is even more difficult given the individualistic ethos of so many people. This problem is exacerbated by the importance many writers assign to what was a very minor point for Smith: the invisible hand.

THE INVISIBLE HAND

Smith used the term "invisible hand" only once in each of his books. In *Theory of Moral Sentiments*, in a paragraph in which he characterized the rich as being naturally selfish and rapacious, he used the term while referring to landlord-tenant relations, a relic of feudal agriculture, not a market economy (Smith 1790, I 466).

The one use in *Wealth of Nations* is in a chapter on restraints on imports:

> As every individual, therefore, endeavours as much as he can both to employ his capital in the support of domestic industry, and so to direct that industry that its produce may be of the greatest value; every individual necessarily labours to render the annual revenue of the society as great as he can. He generally, indeed neither intends to promote the public interest, nor knows how much he is promoting it. By preferring the support of domestic to that of foreign industry, he intends only his own security; and by directing that industry in such a manner as its produce may be of the greatest value, he intends only his own gain, and he is in this, as in many other cases, led by an invisible hand to promote an end which was no part of his intention. Nor is it always the worse for the society that it was no part of it. (Smith 1791, II 181).

One use in a book as long as *Wealth* should not be taken as Smith endorsing individualism. People in Great Britain in his time were deeply enmeshed in multiple community connections.

That he used this term only three times in a large body of writing, once in each of his books and one time in his other manuscripts, indicates it was not central to his thinking; his use of the term does not justify the emphasis many have placed on it. Indeed, one indication of its insignificance is that some Smith scholars consider the term to be a "mildly ironic joke" (Rothschild 2001, 116).

Editors of a reprint of *Theory* argue that, in Smith's published books, the context for the invisible hand is Stoic harmony in society. They state that the foundation for both of Smith's books was a combination of Stoic and

Christian virtues and that a major source for Smith's Stoic ideas was the Roman connection of moral duties with citizenship (Smith 1976, 7). Such interpretation makes it more about sociability than individualism.

German economists played a large role in distorting Smith's meaning. Their reading of his two works was that he had shifted diametrically from the sociability in *Theory of Moral Sentiments* to individualism in *Wealth of Nations*. This is the "Adam Smith Problem." I cannot explain why Smith was so grossly misunderstood by German economists. The Germans were dialectical thinkers, and dialectics entails a synthesis of two opposites. One would think that their synthesis of individual and community would have been some hybrid (such as Smith's, where liberty and sociability were both important values within his justice, liberty, equality formula). In other words, the individual was important, but so was the community. The mystery is why they missed any dialectical synthesis, and instead emphasized the antithesis. They truncated the dialectical process.

Given the religious temper of Scotland in Smith's time, and given that the "invisible hand" sounds like God is intervening in the market, did he use it for religious insurance? While this might seem out of character, there are reasons for this supposition. People living in the twenty-first century may have difficulty understanding the importance of religion in eighteenth century Scotland. But Gavin Kennedy writes of the threat of religious zealots throughout Smith's life and states that economic explanations had to conform to religious (biblical) doctrines (Kennedy 2010, 8 and 81). Smith himself was not religious, but he observed the religious furor against some of the writings of his close friend, David Hume (see, for instance, his September, 1765 letter to Hume in Mossner 1987, 108). In addition, Smith's beloved mother was deeply religious. In *The Infidel and the Professor*, Dennis Rasmussen wrote of several possibilities, including that "Smith learned a lesson from Hume's encounters with the devout" and that "he wanted to avoid offending his pious mother" (Rasmussen 2017, 16). So it seems possible that he inserted this single reference in *Wealth* for protection against religious zealots.

Kennedy argues that the term invisible hand was a "popular, mainly theological, seventeenth- to eighteenth-century metaphor." And he comments, "Literary metaphors describe but do not exist, though we can imagine their relation to the object they describe. The invisible hand metaphor 'corresponds to nothing in reality,' 'contributes nothing to knowledge,' and, today is a 'distraction and a diversion' in economics. Markets work by visible prices, not by 'invisible hands'" (Kennedy, in Hanley 2016, 467–68; for a more detailed critique of the invisible hand, see Hill 2016, 31–3).

Still, the invisible hand remains a common misinterpretation of Smith's system. Heyne, analyzing economics from a religious perspective, provides an example of such distorted thinking; referring to the invisible hand, he attributed moral suspicion of economics to "the fact that economists specialize in the analysis of social systems that no one controls and that produce results that no one intended" (Heyne 2008, 5). But it is a huge logical leap from market economics to an autonomous system. No social system is self-starting and self-regulating. It takes millions of people, acting in their own interest, for the economic system to function. Assuming otherwise surrenders the field to selfish individualists whose very visible hands manipulate the economy for their own benefit. Promoting the public interest most effectively should include moral/ethical decisions by living, breathing people, not reliance on a mythical invisible hand. "Invisible hand" arguments ignore *Theory of Moral Sentiments* and the ethics/justice emphasis of *Wealth of Nations*.

Sen provides some historic context for the continued misuse of the invisible hand; he writes that "faulty analysis" and "severely selective citations" produced an image of Smith as a "champion of pure market based capitalism":

> That distorted image of Smith, which has been the source of so much abuse of Smith's ideas, would solidify in the century after Smith's death, and it came to be canonized in the twentieth century. It remains the standard understanding of Smith today in mainstream economic textbooks and in daily newspapers. (Sen 2011, 258).

To summarize, the published works of this systems thinker support a balanced view of markets, peopled by individuals with responsibilities for harmonious community, not some otherworldly market regulator. The question for us is whether the visible hands of business will monopolize the economic system or whether the people, represented by a democratic government, will have a role.

The invisible hand was a trivial metaphor for Smith; but he did recognize the very visible hands of merchants in British trade policy. This leads us to mercantilism, a policy that granted a few individuals trade monopolies (for example, the East India Company) and restricted colonial trade to the mother country.

CRITIQUE OF MERCANTILISM

Trade in the eighteenth century was monopolized by colonial powers. French colonies could only trade with France or other French colonies; British colonies could only trade with Britain or other British colonies. Such restricted trade was an important cause of the American Revolution. Smith directly confronted this system, advocating free trade in *Wealth of Nations*. While *Wealth* was published in 1776, the founders were not aware of it until long after July 4. American diplomats in Paris, such as John Adams and Benjamin Franklin, learned of it there, but it took months before the book crossed the Atlantic. Note that Smith was writing the book long before the Declaration of Independence. That the Declaration and *Wealth* were both published in the same year is coincidental; there is no causal link.

While criticizing the restrictive nature of mercantilism, Smith endorsed expanding the benefits of international commerce to a wider community:

> Nations have been taught that their interest consisted in beggaring all their neighbours. Each nation has been made to look with an invidious eye upon the prosperity of all the nations with which it trades, and to consider their gain as its own loss. Commerce, which ought naturally to be, among nations, as among individuals, a bond of union and friendship, has become the most fertile source of discord and animosity. (Smith 1791, II 243–44).

Nations would be better off working together, but instead have been acting unilaterally. The power of Smith's argument has been demonstrated in recent years by the European Union.

Smith was well aware that merchants, a small sector of the population, used their political influence over members of Parliament to profit at the expense of the majority. They secured exclusive rights to colonial trade that harmed consumers and the economy. Note that mercantilism had domestic economic and political costs. He pointed out the negative effects of merchants' interests which are "directly opposite to that of the great body of the people." He caustically criticized "the mean rapacity" of merchants (Smith 1791, II 243–44). Let us reflect on that phrase. In Smith's time, according to the *Oxford English Dictionary*, rapacious referred to excessive greed. Since he was a meticulous craftsman, repeatedly revising his books, it seems quite possible that Smith felt so strongly that he deliberately added "mean" in order to increase the intensity of the already harsh term: rapacity.

As was his style, Smith provided examples of this selfish behavior. For instance, woolen manufactures obtained restrictive legislation that benefited them at the expense of shepherds: "To hurt in any degree the interest of any one order of citizens, for no other purpose but to promote that of some other, is evidently contrary to that justice and equality of treatment which the sovereign owes to all the different orders of his subjects" (Smith 1791, II 504). This is the sociable Smith, criticizing individual greed. In this example, the liberty of woolen manufactures to influence Parliament was criticized because of the injustice and inequality resulting from the legislation they secured. Justice and equality were as important as liberty.

Smith was critical of influential citizens for feathering their nests through political influence. He excoriated mercantilism both for restricting trade and for the unfair influence of the wealthy in government, by which he meant a linkage of "political lobbying, anti-competitive regulation, egregious financial returns, growing inequality and loss of public trust" (Norman 2018, 243). His ideal was widespread wealth, including all classes.

Evensky, writing about *Wealth of Nations,* states that "Smith spends most of Book IV demonstrating that mercantilist policies in fact reduce the wealth of the nation. His objective is to unmask the advocates of these distorting policies as powerful players who use their wealth and influence to persuade or if necessary, 'intimidate the legislature' into adopting their self-serving policies" (Evensky in Hanley 2016, 80). Trade monopolies enriched a few at the expense of producers, consumers, and other traders who were barred from the trade.

Smith wanted the consumer to come first: "Consumption is the sole end and purpose of all production; and the interest of the producer ought to be attended to, only so far as it may be necessary for promoting that of the consumer." Smith considered this to be "perfectly self-evident." However, "in the mercantile system, the interest of the consumer is almost constantly sacrificed to that of the producer" (Smith 1791, II 515). This describes our current CEO-dominated shareholder capitalism. The stakeholder labeled "consumer" is now only a means to the end of more billions for the shareholders.

Our modern form of mercantilism, a system benefitting a few individuals at the expense of the many, contradicts Smith's emphasis on equal justice and liberty. While some phrases in Smith's large corpus of writings may seem to support rugged individualism, one can reach that conclusion only by ignoring his systemic thinking. For example, while he did advocate freeing trade from the shackles of mercantilism, he stated that it should be done cautiously, within the parameters of his "equality, liberty, justice" formula for wealthy, happy nations. Typical of his concern for workers, while he recognized that free trade would increase the volume of international trade, Smith argued that such expansion must be done gradually to avoid depriving "many thousands of our people" of employment (Smith 1791, II 202–3).

COSTS OF DIALECTICAL EXTREMISM

Laissez-faire individualism provides fertile ground for the myth that capitalism requires a survival of the fittest, no-holds-barred free market in which issues like socio-economic justice are irrelevant. Many (but not all) businessmen act as if profit maximization, at any cost, is the only consideration. Thus we see corporations establishing manufacturing facilities in countries where environmental regulations, safety rules, and wages are well below United States' standards. The human cost of such policies, both in the host country and in terms of jobs outsourced from the United States, apparently is not a concern. In short, globalization based on an unfettered free market ideology, a Darwinian economic struggle, has exacerbated social injustices and created new ones, rather than mitigating harm. American capitalists have led this stampede into the Hobbesian jungle, but many other predators have joined in. News media regularly report social injustices by businesses throughout the world. Add to this the gross economic and political inequality in many countries, and one has a recipe for seething frustration that produces terrorists. Free market capitalism reinforces it, but an ethical market capitalism would promote justice.

In no way is this intended as a defense of terrorism, the myth that man can know the will of God and thus can be God's executioner. Nor is it an attack on Islam. Muslim terrorists have no monopoly on usurping God's will for their diabolical purposes. I doubt any religion is free of this particular type of hubris. For many centuries, Christians killed one another, plus Jews, Muslims, and adherents of other religions. Tolerance has been a difficult lesson, one not mastered by many people; repeated acts of bigotry indicate that it has not yet been learned in the United States.

People of religion should not think that tolerance requires them to surrender their faith. Tolerance simply means that no human being can claim the omniscience of the Almighty. Striving to understand the will of the Almighty for one's own life is admirable, but people should respect different revelations received in other cultures. Surely, if the Almighty is not only omniscient but also omnipotent, that power could reveal itself in multiple ways. At any rate, finite human minds cannot be certain that their particular revelation is the only truth. How can anyone absolutely know that the Almighty is not made manifest to others in different ways? How much suffering has been caused by the hubris of people afflicted with certainty they held the truth, even though such absolute knowledge is logically unattainable? In short, there is no religious justification for terrorist acts.

For two centuries, the political economy of the United States has been based on a dialectically extreme, individualistic free market interpretation of Smith's capitalism, with two exceptions: the Progressive Era and the New Deal. The New Deal extended into a long recovery after World War II, but the Chicago school of economists, led by scholars such as Milton Friedman and Friedrich Von Hayek, countered with free market arguments that helped stimulate a resurgence of individualism at the expense of community. As Urbinati explains, Hayek omitted "republican 'ardor' for the public good (of central importance to the American founding fathers)" (Urbinati 2015, 62).

One of the most damaging blows against individuality within communities came from Friedman, with his doctrine of shareholder responsibility. His argument that corporations' main responsibility, maximizing shareholder value, omitted many additional stakeholders (such as workers, consumers, communities hosting corporate facilities, the environment), with predictable harm to stakeholders. One cannot maximize shareholder value without harming others connected to the corporation. If Friedman had instead written "Maximize shareholder and stakeholder value," he would have been in agreement with Smith's "justice, liberty, and equality" formula for the greatest prosperity for all classes (Smith 1791, III 13).

Shareholder value ignores an important part of the "invisible hand" paragraph (quoted earlier): "As every individual, therefore, endeavours as much as he can both to employ his capital in the support of domestic industry, and so to direct that industry that its produce may be of the greatest value; every individual necessarily labours to render the annual revenue of the society as great as he can" (Smith 1791, II 181). Shareholder value is nowhere to be found in that paragraph; capital is to be used to maximize the value of production. There is no mention of profit as a metric for success; but maximizing production in order to increase what we today call gross national product (GNP) is listed. That is the purpose. Pure shareholder value at the expense of justice and equality replaces the purpose of market capitalism—making things and providing services—with the metric of success, profits.

Friedman's advocacy of shareholder capitalism provided academic cover for corporate raiders. Reich notes, "Starting in the 1980s, as a result of the takeovers mounted by [Carl] Icahn and a few other raiders such as Michael Milken and Ivan Boesky, a wholly different understanding about the purpose of the corporation emerged. . . . Raiders targeted companies that could deliver higher returns to shareholders mainly by abandoning their stakeholders" (Reich 2020, 102). The corporate raiders implemented Friedman's idea.

Maximizing shareholder value is biased toward the short term. "Higher profits now" take precedence over sustainable profits for the long term. But who can calculate whether the short term is more valuable? It also seems obvious that maximizing shareholder value shortchanges other stakeholders. For instance, does a corporation focused on shareholder value pay fair prices for valuable resources provided by the community (such as an educated workforce, streets and highways, utilities) and resources extracted from the environment?

Shareholder value is clearly an example of what Aristotle labeled chrematistics, described by Herman Daly and John Cobb as "the branch of political economy relating to the manipulation of property and wealth so as to maximize short-term monetary exchange value to the owner. *Oikonomia*, by contrast, is the management of the household so as to increase its use value to all members of the household over the long run" (Daly and Cobb 1989, 138). The unlimited accumulation inherent in chrematistics "is evidence for Aristotle of the unnaturalness of the activity. True wealth is limited by the satisfaction of the concrete need for which it was designed. For *oikonomia*, there is such a thing as enough. For chrematistics, more is always better" (Daly and Cobb 1989, 139). In short, consistent with Adam Smith's arguments, Daly and Cobb argue that the purpose of economics should be service to the community (Daly and Cobb 1989, 19). Ironically, Friedman's doctrine not only contradicts Aristotle's ideal but also Smith's emphasis on consumers as the purpose of production (see Hill 2016, 21–60 for a detailed discussion of Smith's views on economic justice).

Victor Reuther, interviewed by Studs Terkel, explains what Friedman's doctrine meant for one group of stakeholders:

> The character of corporate America has undergone a change. There were old-line entrepreneurs, who were really interested in running the business and making things the market needed. Now, the money manipulators have taken over. They don't give a damn what they make. If they close the goddamn thing down and buy another oil well, that's okay with them. No amount of wage concessions is going to interest those people.
>
> They don't feel any sense of responsibility to the workers in those valleys in Pennsylvania and Ohio where the steel mills are being shut down. (Terkel 1998, 167).

Shareholder economics has political consequences; floods of money bankroll political campaigns and support think tanks advocating laissez-faire. Presidents from both parties have, in what amounts to democratic malpractice, supported Friedman's approach, favoring one class over the others. We now face the political malady John Adams feared most. Our democratic government of, by, and for the people has been replaced by a plutocracy, yet many people still do not understand the perils of aristocracy that Adams so deeply feared. And many people do not understand that our market system is not the sociable market advocated by Adam Smith but rather a form of the mercantilism he excoriated. Nor does it demonstrate love for one's neighbor.

What then did Smith advocate? Instead of pure liberty, he wanted a market economy that had ethical business practices and allowed equal opportunity, in other words, liberty within boundaries. If businesses ignore justice and equal opportunity, the government should restore balance in the system. Critics will argue that giving the government a larger role will destroy the market economy. Such critics ignore the very real success of multiple European countries that maintain more activist governments and just, egalitarian market economies.

Others will argue that liberty promotes creativity, that constraining it will deprive inventors and entrepreneurs of fair returns for their ingenuity and hard work. This argument might be labeled the "deservingness" argument. It would certainly be contrary to Smith's ideals to deprive people of their just rewards; if someone has invented something truly useful, she deserves to be rewarded. Smith's principles are compatible with financial incentives for creativity. But rewarding creativity is only a minor source of inequality today; much larger sources include stock market manipulation and monopolization of productivity increases by the wealthy, especially through massive CEO compensation packages.

Is it fair that many people become wealthy because of financial manipulation and/or undue influence in executive compensation committees, rather than by creating valuable products? In addition, does the upper class pay fair value for government services, especially since many in the top 1% income bracket pay a lower rate of income tax than the middle class?

On the other side of the coin, millions of workers have been deprived of reasonable compensation. Middle-class and worker incomes have been stagnant for decades while the wealthy, especially the top 1 percent, have seen astronomical increases in income. One important reason for this is a change in the way productivity gains have been distributed in the last fifty years. They have been enormous but have flowed to the rich, in contrast to the immediate post-World War II period when they were shared by all classes. This recent monopolization of productivity gains by the wealthy is completely contrary to Smith.

This is not an argument against wealth. This is not a plea for absolute equality. It is an argument for fairness, for rebalancing the US political economy. A market system with justice, liberty, and equality, which Smith advocated, would be more complex than a system based on liberty alone. It would make the United States a better nation for all its citizens—workers, the middle class, and the wealthy as well. The country would be stronger economically because increasing income inequality in the United States is dampening economic growth (Bivens 2017). See Chapter 5 for substantiation of this point.

None of this is to indicate that Smith was against wealth. He assumed a class system and saw value in the wealthy class providing lower classes something to aspire to. He believed that there should be diffusion of wealth, not concentration. He understood that there would be variations in wealth, but these variations should occur within a context of justice. After all, his book was entitled *Wealth of Nations,* not *Wealth of Individuals.* Also, much of his criticism of mercantilism was directed at the monopolistic practices of wealthy individuals, practices supported and enabled by members of Parliament. If we continue to practice a capitalism that is insensitive to the social justice message of Smith, we will continue to nurture the resentments that provide fertile soil for disorder. We could have a different capitalism that would be consistent with Christian values, the values of America's founders, and Smith. Social justice was an important value for all of these. Combine social justice with the equal liberty of the American Revolutionary Era and love for one's neighbor and one has the recipe for a very different capitalism.

Capitalism in the United States in recent decades has emphasized the autonomous individual acting within a market system, but it has ignored the social justice element of Smith's equation. He saw an important role for government in the economy, and he argued for important benefits for all individuals. His "both-and" arguments for market economies were about individuals acting within communities instead of the "either-or" individualism that prevails today. This community aspect means that Smith's capitalism would be fairer than our current savage capitalism.

CONCLUSION

Smith appreciated legitimate self-interest. He wrote that people "have little respect" for anyone who ignores personal goals that can be attained "without either meanness or injustice. . . . Those great objects of self-interest, of which the loss or acquisition quite changes the rank of the person, are the objects of the passion properly called ambition; a passion, which when it keeps within the bounds of prudence and justice, is always admired in the world" (Smith 1790, I 435–36). Note the qualifier: self-interest with prudence and justice, in short, self-interest within a community context.

These limits are clear to Sen, who notes that Smithian self-interest is an adequate explanation for "what motivates trade and people's inclination to participate in exchange." But it was not intended to apply to "the broader problem of what is needed for a good society, including proper functioning of the market economy" (Sen, 2011, 264). Individuals are expected to compete in order to advance their self-interest in markets, but in a good society that competition would be within the boundaries of justice.

Nelson also argues that economic individualism is not a recipe for a healthy society: "The market must exist within an institutional and civic-value context that transcends individual self-interest and supports and encourages actions that have a wider benefit for the common good" (Nelson 2001, 268).

Our nation was built by people acting for the common good; it has been defended by such cooperation. The economy depends on teamwork. But our country is now suffering because of a distortion of our fundamental values. While some businesspeople understand that profits depend on the interaction of multiple stakeholders and that treating workers well is a profit generator, too many maximize shareholder value, regardless of the impact on workers, host communities, and the environment.

For everyone to have an equal opportunity to pursue the American Dream, we must rebalance our political economy based on what Smith actually wrote. Market fundamentalists abhor government actions to promote a fair economy; they seem unaware that Smith deliberately excluded laissez-faire from *Wealth.* The Invisible Hand is an important part of their free market ideology even though Smith scholars deny its significance. Why do they ignore his repeated advocacy of wealth for all classes and instead emphasize concepts which he used rarely or not at all? Individualistic versions have obscured the community orientation of his justice, liberty, and equality formula. Smith was not against the wealthy; his ideal class system was compact with no huge gaps between classes. That type of class structure existed in the United States after World War II, but we have diverged from it in recent decades.

Rebalancing will be better for all. More equal nations have stronger economies, stay out of recessions longer, and recover from them faster. They also have better health outcomes (in all classes) and score higher in happiness rankings (see chapter 6 for documentation of this point). Wealthy people might also be happier in a more egalitarian society because more money often does not bring more happiness. Smith understood this centuries ago; he argued that the wealthy gain little satisfaction from materialistic consumption and are lacking in happiness. Contemporary happiness scholars support his argument.

To summarize, Smith's market economy included justice and equality in addition to liberty. It could restore the American Dream for all citizens. His ideas have been misunderstood and oversimplified as individualistic capitalism for too long. This is not an argument that self-interest should be ignored; instead, individualism should be dialed back to individuality within myriad social relationships. Remembering Smith's formula for wealthy, happy nations may be the best way to move toward his sociable market system. Ignoring his formula has contributed to immense increases in wealth and power of the few, at the expense of the many, thereby contradicting both the Christian love ethic and impeding attainment of the Founders' desire for a democratic republic. Sociable, moral markets must replace individualistic, amoral free markets.

Liberty today is often crass individualism, which, as manifested in the political-economic system of the United States, impoverishes many of God's children. In contrast to the love ethic and to the commandment to have no other gods before God (Exodus 20:3), shareholder capitalism, the market manifestation of our myth of rugged individualism, is now the god (see Knowlton and Hedges 2021, 224–25),

Walter Rauschenbusch, an early twentieth-century theologian, argued that capitalism "was inimical to Christianity" (Dorrien 2018, 34–5). That is certainly true of the type of capitalism currently practiced in the United States.

So now we turn to Christianity, another major source of our ideals. The next chapter examines the individual/community relationship in Christianity (and other religions).

Chapter Three

Christian Sociability

Individualism, virtually nonexistent in Smith's era, is incompatible with his sociability. It also has no role in Christianity. That was true for Americans of the revolutionary era; according to Barry Shain, they believed in "a life of ordered liberty that was necessarily communal" (Shain 1994, 316 and 324–25). Their community orientation included a "strong sense of personal and political limits derived from the Christian dogma of original sin" (Shain 1994, 320–21). Moreover, the Founders agreed with "Americans of all religious persuasions" who thought that religion "transformed otherwise sinful individuals, creating good citizens who made an orderly society possible" and prosperous (Hutson 2003, 32–3). Revolutionary era Christians were individuals within communities. But how important is sociability in a religion that is based on individual salvation?

INDIVIDUAL SALVATION

One becomes a Christian by making an individual decision to accept Jesus Christ as one's personal savior. Conversion is a personal, not a communal, act. Such individual salvation was a radical challenge to ancient religious traditions. In Rome, religion had been a family decision made by the *paterfamilias*; an individual abandoning the family religion for a different religion had been unheard of (Siedentop 2014, 9). Thus, the Christian idea of individual salvation was revolutionary. Larry Siedentop argues that Paul's vision of universal freedom "amounted to the discovery of human freedom—of a moral agency potentially available to each and every one, that is, to individuals" (Siedentop 2014, 60).

But individual salvation did not leave one bereft of community; it placed one in a new community. Dissolution of traditional social bonds led to "a new basis for human association, a voluntary basis—joining humans through loving wills guided by an equal belief" (Siedentop 2014, 62). Donald Hay makes the same point, commenting on Paul's letter to the Romans: "The new freedom which a man has in Christ has its practical consequences in a life of service to others, both within the Christian community and without." And Hay states "that *ideal* humanity finds its expression not in individualism, but in membership of one another" (Hay 1989, 86). The yin-yang of individuality within community is explicit in Romans 12:4–5: "For as in one body we have many members, and not all the members have the same function, so we, who are many, are one body in Christ, and individually we are members one of another." Individual salvation places one in community.

To be consistent with Jesus' teaching, Paul could not have reached any other conclusion; throughout the Gospels, Jesus emphasized community. Here are two examples supporting this statement, starting with the Great Commandment. Asked by the Pharisees what was the greatest commandment, Jesus responded:

> "You shall love the Lord your God with all your heart, and with all your soul, and with all your mind." This is the greatest and first commandment. And a second is like it: "You shall love your neighbor as yourself." (Matthew 22:37–39).

Taken by itself, the Great Commandment may be interpreted as being compatible with individualism, but the "second is like it" adds a sociable dimension. How can one truly love the Lord with all one's heart, soul, and mind without also fulfilling the second commandment? As W. Russell Pregeant states, "In Jesus's mouth it is a call to a radical egalitarianism that treats all persons as not only of equal worth but of equal standing in the community and before God." And he reinforces the community orientation when he writes about "the pervasive biblical emphasis on human unity and Jesus's rejection of social hierarchies" (Pregeant 2016, 41). These verses are an important source for the love ethic and clearly contradict rugged individualism. Thus, they raise the question whether individualistic, libertarian capitalism is compatible with loving one's neighbor.

The love ethic is an important part of Adam Smith's *Theory of Moral Sentiments.* The editors of an Oxford University Press edition of that work state that his ethical doctrines are a combination of Stoicism and the Christian love ethic (Raphael and Macfie 1976, 6). If you love your neighbor as yourself, you will act in ways that are acceptable to the impartial spectator. But the love ethic goes beyond an individual's process for determining acceptable social behavior. Love requires action. Implementing the love ethic is impossible outside community. Christianity is incompatible with individualism; the remainder of this chapter develops this argument.

Stephan Hart explains it this way: "The love ethic, in short, tells many Christians that we are set on earth to serve each other, not to look out for ourselves; that we should put the needs of others ahead of maximizing our own economic interests; that we should not use others as means but only as ends" (Hart 1992, 96). Similarly, discussing solidarity, Pope John Paul II wrote, "It is, instead, 'a *firm and persevering determination* to commit oneself to the common good; that is to say to the good of all and of each individual, because we are *all* really responsible *for all*'" (Ederer 2011, 137).

That this ethic is quite radical can be seen in the parable that immediately follows the great commandments, the parable of the Good Samaritan, Jesus' answer to the lawyer's question, "Who is my neighbor?" (Luke 10:29–37). A man traveling from Jerusalem to Jericho is attacked and robbed; a priest and a Levite ignore the injured victim, but a Samaritan shows compassion and rescues him. The hero of the story, a loathed enemy, upholds Jesus' command to love one's enemy (Matthew 5:44). As Peter Gomes states, Jesus' definition is "inclusive, even elastic, so that the definition of neighbor knows no limit" (Gomes 2007, 85–6).

This high standard is also clear in Matthew 5:48 where "Jesus counsels his followers to 'be perfect . . . as your heavenly father is perfect,' which in context means to love one's enemies because God causes the sun to 'rise on the evil and the good.' That is to say God treats all persons alike, both the righteous and the unrighteous!" (Pregeant 2016, 281). Similarly, the Golden Rule, "Do to others as you would have them do to you" (Luke 6:31), is the antithesis of individualism. (Similar precepts are found in many religions.)

The societal implications of the Golden Rule were certainly clear to John Adams. He thought that equality meant that all (men) were independent and had equal rights even though they were not equal in abilities. However, Adams also argued that the real equality of Christianity is in the precept "do as you would be done by" (Adams and Adams 1980, 161–62). His invocation of the Golden Rule interprets equality as an active principle; individuals must treat everyone the same (Hill 2007, 38–9). But selfish individualists ignore others by focusing on their own desires; they deprive the unemployed, the underemployed, and the underpaid of opportunities to earn a good life. Tax cuts that gild the lilies of billionaires at the expense of government welfare programs are an example of selfish individualism. Such selfishness is incompatible with equal treatment for all.

Servant leadership is an example of community; Jesus said, "The greatest among you must become like the youngest, and the leader like one who serves" (Luke 22:26). Christ's washing the feet of his disciples exemplifies a nonhierarchical community orientation in which, paradoxically, those who would be leaders must also be servants (Pregeant 2004, 145). And servant leaders have a diverse flock, as Albino Barrera makes clear:

> Thus, note the "unclean" people (e.g., tax collectors) in the table-fellowship of Christ. Moreover, there will be the hungry, the naked and the needy whom disciples should receive gladly and serve (Mt 25:31–46). Such inclusiveness and unconditional welcome for those whom they would have otherwise avoided is an occasion for personal growth and community formation. It is also an important stepping-stone to learning what true love of God and neighbor is. (Barrera 2013, 170).

At least one Republican Senator understood this concept. J. Philip Wogaman reports that Senator Mark O. Hatfield (R-OR) spoke "of the crisis when he came to understand that 'service to others, solely for their own behalf and even entailing deep sacrifice, is the true essence of leadership and the ultimate form of power'" (Wogaman 2000, 234). And it was understood by Pope John Paul II who connected liberty and service: "The freedom with which Christ has set us free (cf. Gal 5:1) encourages us to become the servants of all. Thus the process of development and liberation takes concrete shape in the exercise of solidarity, that is to say in the love and service of neighbor, especially of the poorest" (John Paul II 1987, 37).

The incompatibility of individualism and Christianity was clear to Albert Schweitzer. Although he was successful as a scholar and a concert organist, he decided to devote part of his life to medical mission service in Africa. His life purpose gained clarity when he understood one of Jesus' sayings: "'Whosoever would save his life shall lose it, and whosoever shall lose his life for My sake and the Gospel's shall save it.' Now the answer was found. In addition to the outward, I now had inward happiness" (Schweitzer 1949, 70). As an individual, he gained inner peace by serving others. But one need not be a Schweitzer or a Mother Teresa, serving the less fortunate in Africa or India; there are opportunities for everyone in everyday life, perhaps not on the scale of Mother Teresa, but nonetheless worthwhile.

Contemporary capitalism is the very antithesis of servant leadership. The authors of a recent book on capitalism label our system "plantation economics," which grossly exploits people and resources. "At the intersection of economic and theological understanding is the truth that our present corporate plantation systems are deeply flawed and destructive for all involved, including those at the very top" (Knowlton and Hedges 2021, 1).

Failure to understand that one's individual actions may have harmful community ramifications can be a life-or-death matter, as an October 2020 incident demonstrates. A minister in Maine officiated at a wedding where COVID-19 precautions were ignored. Some wedding attendees had the virus and spread it far and wide; many people not in attendance got the disease from contact with attendees, and several died. Those deaths apparently did not sway the minister who hired a lawyer and emphasized the church's

First Amendment rights. In a Tuesday, October 15, statement, he wrote that the church was taking anti-COVID steps and would continue to hold services. He argued that since the beginning of this country, people of religion had a Constitutional right to meet.

The minister wanted his parishioners to choose liberty, basing his argument on the First Amendment. But are First Amendment rights unlimited? Does liberty include a right to cause others potentially lethal illness, by refusing to wear masks? John Stuart Mill would have answered in the negative: "The only purpose for which power can be rightfully exercised over any member of a civilised community, against his will, is to prevent harm to others" (Mill 2011, 17). No one would say that individual liberty allows one to harm someone else or to take something of value from another person; ordinarily that gets one sent to prison. But the infamous wedding in Millinocket took something very valuable from some people—good health. That does not seem very loving.

This is not solely a governmental issue; it contradicts Christian ethics. How can ignoring COVID-19 precautions be reconciled with the Golden Rule? How can it be reconciled with the commandment to "Love your neighbor as yourself"? Was the minister saying that God wants worshipers to ignore government mask mandates? Was he saying that God wants individuals to have liberty at the expense of harming others? Does liberty trump the Golden Rule?

There are many other examples. Some Evangelicals refuse vaccination based on a religious right to bodily autonomy, a belief one's body is a temple of God (see I Corinthians 6:19). One is certainly free to believe this. But to refuse vaccination because it pollutes God's temple and thus to cause illness or death to someone else seems to me to be sacrilege because that person is also one of God's temples. How can one love one's neighbor as oneself and cause illness and/or death? Also, where in the Constitution is there a right for private individuals to pass death sentences on other private individuals? That the death sentence is not on a specific person does not mitigate the harsh injustice.

Obviously, the anti-vaxxers would not be passing death sentences on specific individuals. But was the Millinocket minister an accessory to several deaths because of his insistence on a particular form of religious celebration—a public meeting? Given that thousands of churches, synagogues, and mosques accommodated government mandates, his insistence on liberty at the expense of many illnesses and deaths has the appearance of using religion for political purposes. I understand there are other religious leaders (not only Christians) who have defied government advice and mandates, to say nothing of political leaders who have emphasized individual liberty at the expense of others. These examples do not seem to indicate any incompatibility between

First Amendment rights and Christianity but rather an individualistic misunderstanding of the love ethic.

In such cases, liberty is assumed to be absolute when it is, instead, the right to participate in a process. Just as we would not want to be harmed by someone else's freedom, our individual liberty should not harm others. The COVID pandemic has demonstrated how difficult it is to implement that principle.

Thus far, this section has emphasized that personal salvation brings the saved individual into community. But some Christians miss that sociability and emphasize individuality; for them, religion is about other-worldly salvation, individual purity, and the afterlife, not about social justice in the here and now. This myth separates religion from the actions of daily life; when that happens, religion reinforces injustice by failing to provide a prophetic critique of contemporary society.

EXCESSIVE INDIVIDUALISM

Unfortunately, in spite of the clear message of individuality in communities throughout the scriptures, seeds that were planted long ago have grown into enormous weeds, distorting Christianity into a grossly individualistic caricature, strangling democracy, community, and economic justice. One seed was planted in the Garden of Eden when Adam and Eve ate the forbidden fruit; this rejection of a specific prohibition was the earliest weed producer. The original sin was an act of freedom, but it can also be seen as an act of individualism separating Adam and Eve from community with their creator.

Personal salvation, a seed planted two millennia ago, produced a weed that grew prolifically in the modern era because of secular fertilization. Brendon Westler argues that Christianity had an important role in the development of individualism but that modern individualism "is both political and secular in ways that are not reducible to its distant Christian roots" (Westler 2018, 758). Siedentop, aware of Christian roots of individualism, criticizes contemporary individualism for its

> retreat into a private sphere of family and friends at the expense of civic spirit and political participation. This weakens the habit of association and eventually endangers the self-reliance which the claims of citizenship require. Both of these heresies focus on the second word of the core liberal value—"equal liberty"—at the expense of the first word. They sacrifice the emphasis on reciprocity—on seeing ourselves in others and others in ourselves—which we have seen to be fundamental to inventing the individual and which gives liberalism its lasting moral value. (Siedentop 2014, 362–63).

Similarly, George Marsden states that Christianity cannot be blamed for excessive individualism: "Christians have traditionally been united in proclaiming that the heart of human sinfulness is the illusion that we can be our own gods, a law unto ourselves, creating and controlling our own reality" (Marsden 1997, 78). He argues that "current philosophies which absolutize the self pose a real danger of fostering lawlessness" (Marsden 1997, 78–9).

Yet Christianity bears some of the responsibility. Some contemporary Christian groups have been infected. A heavy emphasis on attaining eternal life, inherent in some interpretations of salvation, combined with individualism, runs the risk of ignoring the commandment to love one's neighbor. Brian McLaren criticizes this form of individualism: Christianity, over long periods of time, "Instead of being about the kingdom of God coming to earth . . . has too often become preoccupied with abandoning or escaping the earth and going to heaven" (McLaren 2006, 78).

This approach dominated Christianity during the nineteenth century. In contrast, the Social Gospel movement (end of the nineteenth century into the twentieth century) insisted that "every Christian had a dual obligation to himself and to society" (Curtis 1991, 1–2; see also Putnam 2020, 130). That obligation involved responding to gross socioeconomic inequities. As Eugene McCarraher notes, Catholic and Protestant leaders after World War I agreed that society needed "reconstruction" (McCarraher 2000, 33).

In recent years the antithesis of the Social Gospel, the "prosperity gospel" has attracted significant numbers of adherents. John Schneider criticizes this interpretation:

> It is rare indeed to find any mention in the preaching of how the righteous may, like Job, suffer, or the wicked prosper. It is rare to hear chronicled the inequities in our society, or of real compassion for the poor of the world, the evils we have perpetrated on them, or what our obligations to them thus might be beyond telling them, too, to become Christians and prosper. Instead, a spirit of extreme individualism and nationalism seems to prevail in much of fundamentalism and popular evangelicalism. (Schneider 1994, 40).

This version of Christianity seems to ignore James 2:17: "Faith without works is dead." It does the hungry no good to wish them well; they need to be fed. The doctrine of universal sin, that all have fallen, apparently has been forgotten in this type of Christianity.

In addition, two ideas stemming back to the Reformation reinforced individualism: the priesthood of all believers, important for Reformation churches, and the idea that individual Christians can interpret God's word. Luther's translation of the Bible into German democratized access to the scriptures. It was an important step for freedom within community.

However, to assume that anyone can translate the multiplicity of different books of the Bible seems dangerous. It is not simply a matter of the difficulty of translating a document that probably was copied many times, with so many chances that changes could have been introduced, unintentionally, by amanuenses. There is also an issue of cultural context; the Bible was written over many centuries, millennia before the twenty-first century, in societies quite distant geographically and culturally from the United States. It is easy to see how mistranslations could occur. This is not to say that untrained individuals cannot decide for themselves what scriptures mean for them personally. But such individual interpretation can be dangerous when it destroys community.

Fragmentation of denominations is one example of the danger of the priesthood of all believers. I am not arguing that fragmentation is always wrong; I am not arguing for a rollback of the Reformation. A split every few hundred years may be necessary to counter human misinterpretations of God's plan. Luther attempted to remove accretions on Catholicism; it is stronger today because of the Reformation.

But something that is beneficial in moderation can be quite harmful when carried to an extreme. Growing up a Baptist in West Virginia, I observed such an extreme; it was obvious that there were as many varieties of Baptists as Heinz had pickles. While splitting churches is not forbidden by the Bible or by law (such a law would violate the separation of church and state), it weakens churches' ability to fulfill their purpose, in particular ministering to those in need. Building, buying, or renting and maintaining a physical facility for a new church, as well as paying for a minister (usually including a parsonage), even with low ministerial salaries, is expensive. To put it another way, these costs significantly reduce church funds available for good works. This would seem to be contrary to Jesus' warning about false prophets: "You will know them by their fruits" (Matthew 7:16). Do church expenses for facilities and personnel impede good works? It seems that fragmentation undermines the "love your neighbor," community service function of churches.

The reader might object at this point that the author is judging different varieties of Christianity and, in doing so, is violating the Sermon on the Mount precept "Do not judge, so that you may not be judged" (Matthew 7:1). The author is aware that, from the beginning of the Christian Era, there have been diverse opinions as to what is authentic Christianity. Who is to judge whether any new interpretation is good or not? To deal with this dilemma, I propose the love metric. Does the new interpretation make for a more loving community? Does it produce greater good or greater evil?

James Jones's 1978 Guyana murder-suicide is an obvious example of the more sinister side of individual interpretation. Another would be the Ku Klux Klan, members of which used individual interpretation to support their movement (Meacham 2018, 119). Obviously, this use of Christianity to justify abominable acts is abhorrent. Its reign of terror is in stark contrast to Christ's inclusionary love ethic.

Factional interpretation continues today to exclude certain groups. The 2019 debates in the world Methodist community involving same-sex marriage provide an example. It seems that most voters in the General Conference of the United Methodist Church were saying that they knew God's will, that God could not love same-sex couples, and that voting to allow Methodist ministers to officiate at same-sex marriage ceremonies would be wrong. But how can one know that? Isn't this human pride—a manifestation of individualism? This seems to limit the scope of God's love. I suspect that similar examples of this problem can be found in other denominations and other religions.

SECTARIAN TOLERANCE

Certainty that one's religion is the only true religion has killed untold millions and caused immense misery for hundreds of millions of people. The religious wars resulting from the Protestant Reformation, Hindu-Muslim strife at the time of India's and Pakistan's independence from Great Britain (and continuing today at an increasing level of violence), the Holocaust, and internecine Islamic conflict are too many examples of the horror that can result from religious certainty. But only God knows for sure which path is the right path, so people of religion should be tolerant of different sects and different religions.

This should not be difficult for residents of the United States. We have long since overcome the religious rigidity of the initial Massachusetts settlers. A century and a half after the Plymouth landing, the Adams family exemplified the transition, moving from Puritan intolerance to tolerance. In November 1786, Abigail Adams wrote from Europe to a sister in Massachusetts: "The Seas Mountains and Rivers are geographical boundaries, they contract not the benevolence and good will of the liberal mind which can extend itself beyond the limits of Country and kindred and claim fellowship with Christian jew or Turk" (Hogan 2007, VII 392).

Almost a quarter of a century later, in a January 21, 1810, letter to Benjamin Rush, John Adams, in his inimitable style, explained his understanding that Christianity

> is the brightness of the glory and the express portrait of the character of the eternal, self-existent, independent, benevolent, all-powerful and all-merciful Creator, Preserver, and Father of the universe; the first good, first perfect, and first fair. It will last as long as the world. Neither savage nor civilized man, without a revelation, could ever have discovered or invented it. Ask me not, then, whether I am a Catholic or Protestant, Calvinist or Arminian. As far as

> they are Christians, I wish to be a fellow-disciple with them all. (Schutz and Adair 1966, 160).

At the 1820 Massachusetts Constitutional Convention, Adams, a delegate at the age of eighty-five, proposed a religious freedom amendment for all religions, but it did not pass. Toward the end of his life, Adams read widely in the world's major religions; he wrote to a friend advocating universal tolerance, hoping that translations of the Bible would make it available "among all people." In return he hoped that "translations into English and French, Spanish and German and Italian of the sacred books of Persians, the Chinese, the Hindos," would be available so "our grandchildren and my great-grandchildren may compare notes and hold fast all that is good" (Smith 1962, II 1078–79). The Adams family's openness to other religions is a model for the twenty-first century. Jefferson was also tolerant, including Catholics, Muslims, and atheists in the right to liberty of conscience (Hutson 2003, 145).

The Christian love ethic is incompatible with sectarian intolerance and with individualism, but it thrives when there is individuality within community. So now we turn to the Biblical basis for such inclusive tolerance.

From its very first book, the Bible is inclusive of all peoples. For Judeo-Christian religions, community, not individualism, is the ideal. For instance, Adam, in Hebrew, means mankind; it refers to relationships, not individualism (Stein 2008, 9 and 24). David Stein states that the same is true for the feminine version of the Hebrew word (Stein 2008, 24). God's promise to Abraham, "'I will make of you a great nation,'" also had an inclusive aspect: "'I will bless those who bless you, and the one who curses you I will curse; and in you all the families of the earth shall be blessed'" (Genesis 12: 2–3).

This inclusion of all the families of the earth is extended to all of creation by some scholars: "We rejoice in the extension of community among those of our time who have come to reaffirm community with all peoples, with other animals, with all living things, and with the whole earth" (Daly and Cobb 1989, 385). Albert Schweitzer labeled this inclusivity of the love ethic "universality": "The ethic of Reverence for Life is the ethic of Love widened into universality. It is the ethic of Jesus, now recognized as a logical consequence of thought" (Schweitzer 1949, 180). Does that include people of other religions? Has God been revealed to different cultures in different ways? Schweitzer clearly thought God's love ethic has been seen in different lights:

> The Jewish prophets Amos and Isaiah (760–700 BC), Zarathustra (7th century BC), and Kung-tse (560–480 BC) mark the great turning point in the spiritual history of mankind. Between the eighth and sixth centuries BC thinking men belonging to three nations, living in widely separated countries and having no

> relations whatever with one another, rise one and all to the perception that the ethical consists not in submission to traditional national customs, but in the active devotion of individuals to their fellow men or to aims which should produce an improvement of social conditions. In this great revolution begins the spiritual humanizing of mankind and, with that, the civilization which is capable of the highest development. (Schweitzer 1949, 142).

In addition, individuality within communities and concern for social justice is characteristic of the Afro-Caribbean religion, Vodou (see, for example, Desmangles 1992). Were I more familiar with other religions, I would write about them as well. What I know leads me to believe that sociability is consistent with many, if not all, the world's religions. For instance, that Christianity shares the Golden Rule with other major religions is some evidence that community, not individualism, is important in other religions (see Lao-Tzu 2018, 300, for a Taoist version).

Including Judaism, Islam, and Vodou in this argument will grate harshly on the nerves of anyone who believes her religion has absolute truth. But if one assumes God is omnipotent, such inclusiveness is logical. As Peter Gomes puts it, "If God is the God of all, and not just a tribal deity, then God had made provision, not necessarily known to us, for the healing and care of all his creation, and not simply our little part of it" (Gomes 2007, 62–3; see also 41 and 154–55). To assume that God's will is revealed only through one religion is to "restrict the power of the God of all the ages to be present in and through the lives of non-Christians" (Wogaman 2000, 192). Given the finite capacity of the human brain, perhaps it is wise not to attempt to judge the validity of other religious approaches to ultimate truth.

Such universalism is certainly anathema to some, but the universality of "all the families of the earth shall be blessed" leads me to believe that finite humans should not limit the possibilities of the infinite One. How can mere mortals know that God does not want very inclusive community? In short, does God's community include Muslims, Buddhists, Hindus, Taoists, Vodouists, and others? Does a loving, omnipotent God exclude the multitudes who adhere to these faiths? Mere humans cannot evaluate and should not judge. But a loving discernment of the fruits of the religious group would be rational, indeed wise, since charlatans have used religion for various nefarious purposes, ranging from financial scams to murderous Jonestown.

The final command of Jesus to the disciples, according to Matthew 28:19 was to "make disciples of all nations." As Pregeant writes, "the emphasis is on total inclusiveness, not any type of exclusion" (Pregeant 2004, 186–87). He also writes that the Bible is the story of God's working through Israel and the church "to create community solidarity among the peoples of the world" because all humanity is "God's own family" (Pregeant 2011, 17).

Such universalism should make it crystal clear that racism is absolutely incompatible with Christianity. God's family is all-inclusive. The conversion of the Ethiopian Queen's "Secretary of the Treasury" is an example (Acts 8: 26–40). This inclusive message is especially important in the United States today as "Black Lives Matter" reminds us of our failure to eliminate the racist discrimination that W. E. B. Dubois called "one of the greatest challenges—and most enduring exceptions—to America's communitarian ideal" (Putnam 2020, 201). Lest there be any misunderstanding, all lives matter, but by emphasizing "Black Lives Matter," I am emphasizing that it is time to be truly inclusive.

"All nations" means that everybody is included; that means enemies, too. "In Matt 5:48, moreover, Jesus counsels his followers to 'be perfect . . . as your heavenly father is perfect,' which in context means to love one's enemies because God causes the sun to 'rise on the evil and the good.' That is to say, God treats all persons alike, both the righteous and the unrighteous" (Pregeant 2016, 281). This inclusiveness is also clear in the Old Testament: "The alien who resides with you shall be to you as the citizen among you; you shall love the alien as yourself, for you were aliens in the land of Egypt: I am the Lord your God" (Leviticus 19:34). Deuteronomy 10:19, "love the stranger," makes the same point.

Moreover, Pregeant argues that this inclusiveness is compatible with Judaism "because there was a significant strain in Hebrew thought itself that envisioned such inclusion at the time of Israel's restoration." The Magi worshipping "the Christ child is a reflection of this Jewish hope. The fact that worshipers have appeared from among the Gentiles means that the coming age, in which God's salvation will be made available to all, is even now beginning" (Pregeant 2004, 22).

Other contemporary religious scholars agree. Henri Nouwen emphasizes the importance of prayer, the interior life, to keep activism from deteriorating into hatred for the other, forgetting that God loves our enemies, also. Nouwen reflects on Thomas Merton's criticism of the illusion that one can know God. This illusion leads to the very opposite of inclusiveness—exclusion, self-righteousness, and oppression—Auschwitz, Hiroshima, Jonestown (Nouwen 1998, 197). And David Gushee, commenting on the first two chapters of Genesis, argues that, since we are all made in God's image, we are of equal worth. He also writes: "all human beings are kin as all are descendants from Adam and Eve" (Gushee 2020, 34). Adam and Eve were not the progenitors of any particular religion.

Christianity goes beyond tolerance for the other; it requires love. Love for the other, no matter the race, creed, or nationality, seems incompatible with individualism. And it requires justice.

CHRISTIANITY AND JUSTICE

The love ethic requires that Christians strive for justice for all God's children. Note that "all God's children" is universal; that includes the people from all the continents. Jon Meacham makes this point by quoting a Martin Luther King Jr. sermon at the National Cathedral on March 31, 1968:

> "We are tied together in the single garment of destiny, caught in an inescapable network of mutuality," King said. "And whatever affects one directly affects all indirectly. For some strange reason, I can never be what I ought to be until you are what you ought to be. And you can never be what you ought to be until I am what I ought to be. This is the way God's universe is made; this is the way it is structured." (Meacham 2018, 245).

King's quest for freedom encompassed a broad community, not limited to one race. This is clear in his description of nonviolence in *Stride Toward Freedom*; it might mean going to jail, even death: "But if physical death is the price that a man must pay to free his children and his white brethren from a permanent death of the spirit, then nothing could be more redemptive" (King 1958, 216). Note: the Civil Rights Movement was also about freeing white people! No one of us is free as long as one of us is enslaved.

The inclusiveness of King's thought is clear in his last book. Commenting on "fears, prejudice, pride and irrationality," he wrote that "dark and demonic responses will be removed only as men are possessed by the invisible inner law which etches on their hearts the conviction that all men are brothers and that love is mankind's most potent weapon for personal and social transformation" (King 1967, 101). The love in King's thinking is universal.

His emphasis on justice is supported by scripture. The Hebrew prophets were caustic in their criticism of socioeconomic injustice. Justice is also a strong component of the New Testament message. For example, quoting Galatians 6:10, Pregeant notes that concern for the welfare of the whole human community is clearly stated by Paul with his "injunction to 'work for the good of *all,* and especially for those of the household of faith'" (Pregeant 2011, 108). Many religious leaders are true to the prophetic tradition, providing trenchant critiques of socioeconomic problems. But for such critiques to be consistent with Judaism and Christianity, they must have two characteristics: they must stem from a universal love ethic and be tempered by awareness that one is not omniscient.

This inclusiveness covers all the nations of the world and all socioeconomic classes. As McLaren puts it, "Jesus' secret message in word and deed makes clear that the kingdom of God will be radically, scandalously inclusive. As we've seen, Jesus enjoys table fellowship with prostitutes and drunks, seeming to shift the locus of spirituality from the temple (which he says will be destroyed) to the table of fellowship and reconciliation" (McLaren 2006, 94).

Pregeant connects the Golden Rule, the great commandment, and the beatitudes, writing that they aim for justice (Pregeant 2004, 56). He develops this thought in a more recent work:

> The so-called Golden Rule helps make the love command concrete, as does Matthew's description of the last judgment in 25:31–46, where the criterion for entering eternal life is whether one has performed deeds of mercy. To love is to treat other persons *as persons*, meeting their needs as we would like to have our own needs met. It also means recognizing the inherent worth of others and never treating them as means toward an end. (Pregeant 2011, 106).

But people often cite scripture to avoid doing the justice that God requires. Such proof-texting is a form of misinterpretation that takes some words out of context in an attempt to justify personal views. The very week I am writing this, a letter to the editor of the *Boston Globe* cited an often proof-texted verse, Matthew 26:11: "The poor you have with you always." The common anti-poor interpretation of this verse completely ignores the context.

Jesus was on his way to Jerusalem and certain death. A woman anointed him with expensive oil, which the disciples complained could have been sold to provide relief for the poor. But he saw the anointment as preparation for his burial. When he no longer was with the disciples, they could serve the poor. Mark's version is very clear on this: "But Jesus said, 'Let her alone; why do you trouble her? She has performed a good service for me. For you always (*pantote)* have the poor with you, and you can show kindness to them whenever you wish; but you will not always have me.'" (Mark 14:6–7; see also John 12:8). It is important to note that the sentence, in Greek, is in the present tense (Pregeant 2023, 26).

The translation of the Greek word *pantote* is vitally important for understanding this verse. A New Testament scholar explained to me that the word "usually translated as 'always' just doesn't MEAN 'forever.' *Pan* means all or every, and *tote* means 'when,' 'then,' or 'at that time.' So in the verse, the meaning is not that poverty is ineradicable, but that since the poor are around at any time, you can help them whenever you want to" (e-mail from Pregeant, October 4, 2020). The disciples understood one of Jesus' basic justice messages of concern for the least, the downtrodden, the outcast, but misapplied that lesson in this situation. In no way was he stating a principle of ignoring the needs of the poor; such an interpretation contradicts his consistent message of justice.

Pregeant writes that this story, taken out of context, is often used as justification for extreme neglect of the rights of the poor to life, liberty, and the pursuit of happiness. He adds that anti-poor sermons and the prosperity gospel amount to democratic malpractice because the rights of tens of millions of people are ignored while the rich get richer (e-mail from Pregeant, August 8, 2019). He argues:

> The religious community is not an avenue through which individuals may develop their self-defined potentials, pursue their self-defined goals, and fill their self-defined needs. It is rather a foretaste of a whole new world and as such the revolutionary cadre through which God is able to bring about possibilities the world itself can scarcely imagine. (Pregeant 2022, 199).

In addition, Edith Rasell notes an Old Testament commandment, attributed to Moses, that mandates anti-poverty action (Rasell 2022, 76). "Since there will never cease to be some in need on the earth, I therefore command you, 'Open your hand to the poor and needy neighbor in your land'" (Deuteronomy 15:11). She also argues that working together, not individual competition, is needed to solve our economic problems. "We need a world based on solidarity, not greed. God's reign is one of abundance and sharing, not scarcity and competition" (Rasell 2022, 248–49).

There is no justification for using scripture to ignore contemporary poverty; that would contradict the concern for the poor that is prominent in both the Old and New Testaments. Justice is a central theme of the scriptures. For instance, the Sojourners group, based in Washington, DC, has identified two thousand Biblical verses dealing with God's justice for the poor (Taylor 2020).

By now, it must be clear that Christianity and individualism are incompatible. But there is another factor that Christians should consider. Martin Luther King Jr.'s understanding of personality makes it evident that individualism is not an option for a Christian. He saw human personality as "'something of a great triangle,' creatively integrating personal, social and ultimate concerns: 'At one angle stands the individual person, at the other angle stand other persons, and at the top stands the Supreme, infinite Person, God. These three must meet in every life if that life is to be complete'" (Dorrien 2018, 286).

The United States is a nation with a wide variety of religions that also advocate loving and just communities.

JUSTICE IN OTHER RELIGIONS

Inclusive justice is also evident in Judaism and Islam. Judaism, with ideals such as the Jubilee year (even though there is no certainty it was ever practiced) and Islam, with its requirement of Zakat and prohibitions against interest (even though that has been extremely problematic in real world application) share an emphasis on justice.

The Jubilee year required the economic playing field to be leveled every fifty years. A family, putting up their farm as collateral for a loan and losing it when unable to repay the mortgage, would regain their farm in the Jubilee year. Also, the prophets in ancient Judaism were absolutely clear in their condemnation of injustice; for instance, Pregeant notes prophetic teachings that are harsh indictments: Isaiah 3:10; Proverbs 1:11–19; Amos, and Micah. The Lord requires one to "do justice, and to love kindness" (Micah 6:7). Pregeant's main point is this: "religious devotion means nothing apart from doing justice to one's neighbor" (Pregeant 2016, 104–5).

A. James Reichley, referring to the Founders of this country, argues that Judaic scriptures and rabbinic writings were important sources for their beliefs about justice within communities. These ideas include:

> the unique and equal value of each human life; the root of community in God's covenant with His people; maintenance of social order through rule of law . . .; the injunction to improve the earth through work; the imperative of social justice; and the community's obligation to care for "the stranger, the fatherless, and the widow." (Reichley 2001, 182).

Albino Barrera states that there is virtual consensus among biblical scholars on the "central importance of care for the poor in Old Testament law" (Barrera 2013, 253; see also 254). Referencing Genesis 1:28–30, he emphasizes justice when he writes that "preferential treatment is founded on the very nature of God . . . economic poverty . . . is abhorrent to God. . . . Destitution is a jarring contrast to God's gift of material plentitude when the fruits of the earth were entrusted to human stewardship" (Barrera 2013, 207). Justice extends to one's enemies. Referring to Exodus 23:4, "When you come upon your enemy's ox or donkey going astray, you shall bring it back." Barrera writes that this "duty to help an enemy's farm animals in distress or at risk . . . is a pointed reminder of a deeper underlying obligation to prevent harm" (Barrera 2013, 69).

These scholars are only three of many who could be quoted on the importance of justice in Judaic sacred writing.

Social justice is important in Islam, as well as Judaism and Christianity. Skeptics will scoff at that statement because of the horrors committed by violent Muslims. One cannot deny the terrible violence of Hamas or of radical jihadis, often killing other Muslims simply because they adhere to a different sect, but it must be emphasized that Muhammad distinguished between violent jihad and the greater jihad—the individual's struggle to follow God's commands (Hill 2013, 14). It must also be noted that a very small percentage of the 1.8 billion Muslims in the world are perpetrators of violence.

Individuals are valued within a community context. But some might argue that many Muslim majority countries are dictatorships, that the religion is conducive to tyranny. Noah Feldman notes that Islam "implies no subjugation of one person to any other. The word implies, rather, a recognition of God's ultimate sovereignty that places all people on equal footing before the divine Majesty." Feldman also recognizes that Muslims are equals "in the creation of the Muslim community" (Feldman 2003, 20–1). Dictatorships in Islamic countries are perversions of Islam.

Others might object that Islam has been very intolerant; one has no individual right to believe in a different sect or a different religion. According to Bernard Lewis, such intolerance is aberrant in Islamic history; occasionally, forced conversions did occur and there was persecution of Sunnis, Shia, and Sufis. "But broadly speaking, the use of force, against deviants as against *dhimmis* [believers in other protected religions], was rare, atypical, and due to special circumstances" (Lewis 1998, 124).

The Koran emphasizes justice to other people, as is clear in Surah 5: "Believers! Be resolute in your allegiance to God, staunch witnesses for justice. On no account let hatred against any people cause you to be perverted from what is just. Deal justly. To do so is the nearest thing to the fear of God." Surah 53 states that God punishes evil and rewards good (Cragg 1988, 181 and 283). Equality is inherent in justice, and equality before God is a central concept of Islam, a concept it shares with the other monotheistic religions. Kenneth Cragg also explains that mistreating someone violates that person's rights and offends God (Cragg 1988, 181 and 283).

But what about injustice to women in some Muslim communities? Here one must distinguish between male chauvinism and what Muhammad advocated. His message was progressive with its emphasis on justice, its assault on Meccan polytheism, and its criticism of false contracts, bribery, abuse of women, and socioeconomic inequality (Esposito 1991, 9 and 31). However, both R. Stephan Humphreys and Bruce Lawrence agree that the Koran and Islamic law are patriarchal, and today in many Islamic societies, misogyny, patriarchal interpretations by Muslim theologians, plus questionable traditions attributed to the Prophet, have undermined the just treatment of women called for by the Koran (Humphreys 1999, 224, and Lawrence 1998, 109–48). Islam, Judaism, and Christianity all aim for a just community but have failed to live up to their ideals.

CONCLUSION

Individuality within communities is an important component in three monotheistic religions. Paul Heyne questions whether such sociability is compatible with capitalism. Referring to the Golden Rule, he writes, "If that is indeed, as Jesus says in Matthew, 'the law and the prophets,' it does seem that a commercial society is fundamentally incompatible with Biblical ethics" (Heyne 2008, 74). Heyne is right to state that the individualistic, libertarian capitalism of the United States in the twenty-first century is incompatible with the love ethic. But Smith advocated a sociable capitalism that is compatible with Christianity's love your neighbor commandment.

Individualism contradicts Christian values and starkly contrasts with the equal, just, and sociable market of Adam Smith. Let us now examine whether individualism also contrasts with the individuality within community orientation of the Founders of this nation, the subject of the next chapter.

Chapter Four

John Adams, Factionalism, and the Common Good

This chapter is too short to evaluate the entire life and contributions of a person as complex and controversial as John Adams. The goal, instead, is to explain a danger he foresaw—that factionalism could destroy democracy. In other words, this chapter examines a flaw in our political system that Adams warned about, and which other revolutionary era leaders did not understand. They misinterpreted his warnings as an attack against democracy. The United States was a democratic republic. What was Adams worried about? He feared that a faction he called "the aristocracy" would overwhelm the community.

The Declaration of Independence, the preamble to the Constitution, and the United States motto (*E pluribus unum*) are consistent in their emphasis on the common good. This is not surprising, given that individualism was virtually unknown in the eighteenth century.

According to Barry Shain, individualistic "idiosyncratic attitudes" describe "a dozen or so elite nationalists, mostly in the early national period (after 1790). They do not capture the aspirations and goals of most Revolutionary-era Americans" (Shain 1994, xvi; see also 169–81 *et passim*). The Founders were certainly strong individuals, but they did not intend to promote individualism. They valued their individuality within the context of multiple overlapping communities. Leaders were able to mobilize people because of an extensive community network (Richardson 2023, 173).

Let us first examine the Declaration of Independence and then the preamble to the Constitution to explain this both-and approach.

REVOLUTIONARY-ERA LIBERTY

Our Founders were not revolutionary in the Marxian class struggle sense; nonetheless, they were revolutionary in attempting to establish a democracy in such a geographically extensive area, something that had never before been accomplished. In addition, they were truly revolutionary in declaring that all had an equal and inalienable right to life, liberty, and the pursuit of happiness. They certainly valued economic liberty. After all, that was one of the most important reasons they fought for independence. But the Founders lived at a time when liberty was firmly embedded within community. They did not approve of individualism as we know it today.

John Adams knew that democratic governments were fragile; in a September 27, 1808, letter to Benjamin Rush, he wrote:

> I believe, with you, "a republican government," while the people have the virtues, talents, and love of country necessary to support it, "the best possible government to promote the interest, dignity, and happiness of man." But you know that commerce, luxury, and avarice have destroyed every republican government. (Schutz and Adair 1966, 119–20).

His understanding was based on deep historical knowledge of the fate of democracies and should be a warning for us today. The concerns he listed are examples of individualism undermining the republic, the community.

Throughout this chapter, I will use John Adams as an example of individuality within communities. While Washington, Jefferson, and Franklin are familiar names for most Americans, few today know much about the man called "The Atlas of American Independence" by his contemporaries. But he was highly respected by many in the revolutionary generation. He was a major participant in Continental Congress debates leading to the Declaration of Independence; according to a recent scholar, "By dint of achievement and sacrifice, John Adams was the most important American political leader of his time" (Staloff 2005, 134). During the Revolutionary War, he served as a diplomat in Europe, securing crucial loans from the Netherlands and serving on the team that negotiated the Treaty of Paris.

While he had disagreements with other leaders, such as Jefferson and Hamilton, the differences were over what was best for the nation. They put the nation first, as their service in the struggle for independence demonstrates. Their individuality was within the context of concern for the greater good.

The Founders believed everyone had a responsibility to the community; this is clearly stated by Adams in a letter to his son Thomas: "We are not born for ourselves alone, Benevolence is really a part of our Nature, as self-Love, and man is never so happy as when he is conscious that he is useful to others" (Hogan 2005, VII 440). Citizens were expected to have public spirit, which meant one should sacrifice individual desires for the common good. The public interest was very important to Adams; he wrote that if the people did not have "a positive passion for the public good," there could be no real liberty (Taylor 1979, IV 124–25).

He exemplified that passion. Adams had been the most successful lawyer in Massachusetts (which at that time included Maine); he gave up a lucrative law practice to serve the new nation. His public service in the Continental Congress and as a diplomat in Europe meant long periods of time away from his family, law practice, and farm. Any person with talents needed by the community was expected to sacrifice private interests for the public good. This included paying taxes; "No taxation without representation" was the slogan, not "No taxation." Hiring accountants, lobbyists, and lawyers to avoid taxes and gain special tax treatment would have been incomprehensible to that generation. In fact, notable founders, like Adams and Jefferson, advocated progressive taxes.

None of this means that personal perspectives were ignored. As Adams put it, personal proposals could be submitted to the community for a majority decision, but once that decision was made, "it is the Duty of every Individual to submit to the Decision of the majority although it be against his own opinion or quit the Club" (Lint 2006, XIII 512). Our Founders considered individualism, as we know it today, to be a vice. Good government prevented anarchic licentiousness. The Founders wanted liberty; they also wanted limited government to check what many today see as freedom, but they saw as license (Hill 2007, 40–1).

Adams was known for strong opinions and willingness to support unpopular ideas. He supported independence when many delegates to the Continental Congress were dubious. His logical argumentation was central to the final debate on the issue. Note that his individuality was in service to the wider community, first Braintree, then Massachusetts, and finally the new nation. The public good trumped personal advantage. Such public service was connected to religion, according to Page Smith, author of a two-volume biography of Adams. He argues that Adams converted the concept of original sin into political terms; self-interest was sin while public service was sanctification (Smith 1962, I 234–35). Other Founders shared with Adams an emphasis on the importance of public service (see Hill 2007, 83–90).

This argument does not mean that all people in the revolutionary era fit this description. Even during the war for independence, there were war profiteers, but they were the exception. Independence was won because so many people from all classes acted for the common good. But after the war was won, the exceptions gradually became the rule; individualism subverted the meaning of the Declaration of Independence. Words and phrases in the preamble, such as "liberty," and "all men are created equal" were taken out of historical context. The title of the document does not refer to individual freedom; the signers wanted the thirteen united colonies to be independent of George III. Phrases such as "one people" make it clear that this document was not a manifesto for individualism.

The thirteen colonies were a diverse community; New England Puritans, Dutch New Yorkers, Pennsylvania Quakers and Germans, Maryland Catholics, and others pulled together to win independence. This is not to imply that the process was smooth. United, they defeated the powerful British Empire.

There is always a tension between personal desires and the common good, but we are all better off when we work together. Victory in the Revolutionary War, resulting in immense societal and individual benefits, is an example for contemporary Americans that we all gain from cooperation. Borrowing words from the Declaration, it is our "duty" to "throw off" discriminatory aspects of government that deny rights to anyone in this country. We should model ourselves on our Founders, for their willingness to sacrifice life and fortune for important principles, even though they failed to address equality for all. We should honor them by completing the unfulfilled promises of the Declaration.

GROWTH OF INDIVIDUALISM

The values of the Declaration supported Americans throughout the long Revolutionary War. Thirteen colonies won independence, but afterward it was important to establish legitimacy as one nation, not an easy task given the varied interests of the confederated states.

Diminished concern for community was noted soon after the peace treaty ended the Revolutionary War; Adams and his correspondents commented on an increasing emphasis on private interest at the expense of community. His understanding of the common good was stated in a July 11, 1783, letter to Robert Morris:

> All depends, however, upon the Measures to be taken by Congress and the States for ascertaining their Debts and a regular discharge of the Interest . . . The Ability of the People to make such an Establishment cannot be doubted: and the Inclination of no Man who has a proper Sense of publick Honour can be called in Question. The Thirteen States in Relation to the discharge of the Debts of Congress must consider them Selves as one Body, animated by one Soul . . . The Stability of our Confederation at home, our Reputation abroad, our power of Defence, the Confidence and affection of the People of one state towards those of another all depend upon it. Without a Sacred Regard to publick Justice no Society can Subsist. it is the only Tie which can unite Mens Minds and Hearts in pursuit of the common Interest. (Lint 2010, XV 101).

After Adams wrote this, he received letters from his friends in the United States warning him that public justice and the common interest were not the first concerns of many citizens. William Gordon wrote to him on June 28, 1783: "One great evil among us is, that persons will not unite their endeavours to serve the public cause. Each is busy in attending to his own adventure, not considering that if the ship is lost they must all suffer." Later in the letter he added: "Bad unprincipled men with craft & abilities, unless there are capable men of approved characters & in the esteem of the country to counteract them, will soon run us upon rocks & quicksands" (Lint 2010, XV 68–9).

Gordon's letter was written two weeks before Adams's letter, but because of the long sea voyage, Adams certainly did not receive it until after he wrote his July 11 letter to Morris. In a September 10, 1783, letter to Gordon, Adams wrote: "In all domestick Disputes I wish our countrymen, may moderate their passions, & manifest as much mutual forbearance as possible. I dread the course of our elections if parties prevail" (Lint 2010, XV 277). On November 23, 1783, Elbridge Gerry wrote to warn about some citizens "of ambitious and perhaps envious principles who think 'all made for one, not One for all'" (Lint 2010, XV 369).

Three years later, Adams's correspondents seemed even more concerned; on April 7, 1786, Charles Storer did not write of "some citizens" as Gerry had written; he saw the problem as universal.

> I wish, Sir, there was a little more of that enthusiastic, public spirit remaining, which has supported us thro' a difficult and dangerous war—I think it would be better for us: we are getting too easy & indifferent to the general weal—Private Interest seems to have taken possession of every Individual; and that virtuous patriotism, which was once our boast seems now to be altogether dead. (Lint 2016, XVIII 236).

Two months later John Jay wrote pessimistically about national government finances because the people were "intent on private gain & too inattentive to national Concerns & exigencies" (Lint 2016, XVIII 334).

While Adams's political prescriptions continued to emphasize community over individual, "his political opponents were moving in the opposite direction" (Ryerson, 2016, 335). At least one man of religion reinforced this individualism. In "A Liberal Man's Confession of Faith," Elihu Palmer wrote that he believed that "every man should do just as he pleases." His religious views resulted in his expulsion from Philadelphia, but he continued to preach in other places (Hogan 2009, IX 287).

Under the Articles of Confederation, each state could prioritize their own interests at the expense of the nation; for example, failure of several states to pay their portion of Revolutionary War debts impeded trade. The national government authorized diplomats to negotiate commercial treaties with European and African nations, including attempts to end Barbary States' piracy that was enslaving our seamen and harming commerce. But as the *Papers of John Adams* make clear, Adams's and Jefferson's attempts to complete their diplomatic tasks were complicated by the debt repayment issue (Lint 2016, XVIII throughout). Nationalist leaders understood that government was not the enemy of liberty; they also understood that weak government undermined international trade. This was an important factor in the decision to replace the Articles of Confederation with a new constitution.

The Constitution, negotiated in secret but debated and ratified by the people, provided for a stronger national government. The Preamble to the Constitution, listing the purposes of this new system, is incompatible with individualism.

> "to form a more perfect union": this addressed the imperfection of the "every state for itself" confederation. The weak central government of the Articles of Confederation was replaced by a more powerful federal government. The states remained, but the union of states, the national community, was strengthened.
>
> "establish justice": for the founders this meant ethics as well as the legal system; both inherently involve multiple relationships, not individualism.
>
> "insure domestic tranquility": law and order was certainly part of this. But, with the example of Shay's Rebellion fresh in their minds, the founders knew that an unjust political economy would cause domestic unrest.
>
> "provide for the common defense": this is *sine qua non* for all nations; one person cannot do this alone. None of the thirteen colonies was strong enough to gain or maintain independence separately; freedom required unity, a community of states.
>
> "promote the general welfare": opens the door for a large government role. Do not give a 21st century interpretation to these words. The founders had no conception of a modern welfare system for the indigent; for them, welfare meant the well-being of all. (In the 18th century, this applied only to white males, but the words invite greater inclusivity; we have unfinished business.)
>
> "and secure the blessings of liberty to ourselves and our posterity": this emphasizes community inclusive of future generations. It is notable that "posterity" has been ignored for decades; government policies (e.g., ignoring global warming, underfunding infrastructure, tax policies that leave large debt burdens for future generations) have violated this important point.

None of the purposes can be construed as advocating that people do their own thing. Individualism was something the founders did not endorse. Jefferson wrote that, while we are concerned for our own welfare, nature has also given us "'a love of others, a sense of duty to them, a moral instinct, in short which prompts us irresistibly to feel and to succor their distresses'" (Pangle

1993, 251). In a brief explanation of why he would sign the new Constitution, Benjamin Franklin showed a subtle balancing of individual and community:

> "Thus I consent, sir, to this Constitution because I expect no better. . . . The Opinions I have had of its Errors, I sacrifice to the Public Good . . .
>
> "I cannot help expressing a Wish, that every Member of the Convention, who may still have Objections to it, would with me on this Occasion doubt a little of his own infallibility, and to make *manifest* our *Unanimity*, put his Name to this instrument." (Boorstin 1966, 97–8).

Such willingness to compromise demonstrates a community orientation that did not detract from Franklin's personality. His willingness to "doubt a little of his own infallibility" is still a wise approach today.

John Jay, as Supreme Court chief justice, wrote of the interdependence of individual and national prosperity and the importance of "a well-organized, vigorous government." And he wrote that liberty was not "unlicensed indulgence," that it was secured by "forming a common interest with all the other members of the society" (Lerner 1979, 100). This is individuality within communities. Shain notes that "in spite of the efforts of an influential circle of the Framers, who had hoped to imbue it with a moderately individualistic political philosophy," the Constitution "was predominantly concerned with guarding the public's, not the individual's welfare and interests" (Shain 1994, 31).

The United States had a great advantage in that George Washington, its first president under the new Constitution, was a war hero who was seen by most as being above politics. But while replacing the Articles of Confederation with the Constitution strengthened the nation at the expense of the states, his presidency did not end divisiveness. As Paul Varg notes, "Foreign policy questions during the presidency of Washington became the focal point of political debate and contributed in a major way to the rise of political parties. The Constitution did not envision parties, and Washington was strongly averse to their becoming a part of the American political scene" (Varg 1963, 70). But political parties—factionalism—did become a major problem.

FACTIONALISM

James Traub writes that the Founders were united in their distrust of political factions, what we today call parties, believing they "were inimical to republican government, on the grounds that they served as vehicles for selfish or sectional interests as opposed to national and collective ones" (Traub 2016, 233). Factionalism is criticized in this work as a variant of individualism, in this case a focus on a smaller group at the expense of a more inclusive community.

The Founders' animosity toward faction was consistent with the reasoning of British political philosophers of that era. For instance, Dennis Rasmussen writes that "In Hume's view, 'factions subvert government, render laws impotent, and beget the fiercest animosities among men of the same nation, who ought to give mutual assistance and protection to each other'" (Rasmussen 2017, 26). In a February 1774 letter criticizing Benjamin Franklin as a factious man, Hume sought details about an accusation that Franklin had "surreptitiously sent back to Boston some letters from Thomas Hutchinson, the royal governor of Massachusetts, in which Hutchinson advocated the use of force against" Massachusetts. "'Pray, what strange Accounts are these we hear of Franklyn's Conduct?' Hume inquires. 'I am very slow in believing that he has been guilty in the extreme Degree that is pretended; tho' I always knew him to be a very factious man, and Faction, next to Fanaticism, is, of all passions, the most destructive of Morality'" (Rasmussen 2017, 157).

Adam Smith, a good friend of Hume, had a similar view:

> A true party-man hates and despises candour; and, in reality, there is no vice which could so effectually disqualify him for the trade of a party-man as that single virtue. The real, revered, and impartial spectator therefore, is, upon no occasion, at a greater distance than amidst the violence and rage of contending parties. To them, it may be said, that such a spectator scarce exists anywhere in the universe. Even to the great Judge of the universe, they impute all their own prejudices and often view that Divine Being as animated by all their own vindictive and implacable passions. Of all the corrupters of moral sentiments, therefore, faction and fanaticism have always been by far the greatest. (Smith 1790, I 386).

John Adams had long been deeply concerned by factionalism, but by the mid-1780s, according to Richard Ryerson, he became aware of the faction that he labeled aristocrats. The issue for Adams was preventing them from undermining the republic while using them for the good of the nation. He did not expect the new nation to be a classless society; his main goal for the government was "the security and happiness of the whole society including its weakest members" (Ryerson 2016, 268–69). Aristocracy would be the bane of Adams's existence for the rest of his life. He feared that the new aristocrats would destroy American democracy; political opponents misinterpreted his concern. This led to perhaps the earliest use of "fake news" in our national elections and to Adams's defeat in his bid for reelection.

President Trump was fond of labeling inconvenient truths "fake news." But this is not a new phenomenon; in other times, it was called spin or propaganda. However, there is a difference in degree; today we are exposed to an overflowing fountain of sources. Like earlier generations, we must sort fact from fiction because failure to expose "fake news" can have serious long-term consequences for democracy. For instance, its use as a campaign scare tactic in the 1800 presidential election, one of the dirtiest in United States history, reshaped our political system; political party, faction, not the common good, has dominated since then.

So why did our second president win only one term? Part of the story involves his actions as president. Jeffersonians saw Adams as a Federalist, but Adams believed he acted impartially for the good of the nation, often against the policy preferences of the Federalist leader, Alexander Hamilton. Doing this probably cost him reelection; if Hamilton had supported Adams, he might have defeated Jefferson. Note that the disagreements were about what would be the best policies for the nation.

Hamiltonian Federalists had pushed for war against France because of the XYZ Affair, the attempted bribery of American diplomats sent to Paris to resolve the dispute about French capture of American merchant ships. Adams, as president, prepared for war while engaging in diplomacy to resolve the issue, thereby preventing the crisis from becoming a full-scale war, one the infant United States probably would have lost. Darren Staloff credits Adams with enlightened statesmanship and writes, "This feat was all the more remarkable given the rancorous partisanship within the government and the disloyalty of his own cabinet" (Staloff 2005, 207). The differences between Adams and Hamilton on this issue were enormous, but it must be noted that both were trying to protect the nation.

News of the diplomatic solution did not reach New York until a few days after the election. It is impossible to know whether Adams would have been reelected, had that news arrived before the election. Perhaps it would not have mattered because Aaron Burr had built a powerful Jeffersonian political machine in New York.

The vote in New York may well have had less impact on the result than the Jeffersonian tarring of Adams with the brush of aristocracy. Some even thought that he wanted to establish himself as monarch, so that John Quincy Adams could inherit the throne. Such canards were fake news; John Adams was consistently a supporter of democracy, but he did two things that gave many Americans reason to question whether his long diplomatic sojourn in Europe had changed the stalwart democrat into a believer in aristocracy. His book, *A Defence of the Constitutions of Government of the United States of America* (1787), and his actions as vice president, especially the "titles" controversy, raised suspicions and thus require explanation.

In *Defence of the Constitutions,* Adams argued that the new American democracy would be subject to the same strife among the One (Monarchy), the Few (Aristocracy), and the Many (Democracy) that had affected democratic republics since the ancient Greeks. Based on extensive reading, he argued that democracy was fragile and easily overpowered by the aristocrats. Staloff explains what Adams meant by "aristocrats": "They were those individuals whose prominence, prestige, and power allowed them to influence public opinion and the course of government" (Staloff 2005, 187).

Among other reasons for writing *Defence,* he was trying to warn Americans that without a strong president to counter the few, the new democracy would succumb to aristocratic rule. He was prescient in his fear of the governmental dysfunction we are currently experiencing. His fact-based argument fell on deaf ears. It conflicted with a core American belief: American exceptionalism. Also, his use of the ancient division of governments into the One, the Few, and the Many (Monarchy, Aristocracy, Democracy) was easily distorted into advocacy of an anti-democratic system (Hill 2007, 176–80).

A modern reader might wonder why he used the term "aristocracy." *Defence* was written for both Europeans and Americans. Europeans would understand the term, but Americans misconstrued it as advocating imposition of the old-world system of inherited titles on our new democracy. Instead, he used it in the generic sense of any successful businessman or military, religious, or academic leader, anyone who could control votes in addition to his own. With hindsight, one might wonder why he used a term so laden with memories of the British class system. His explanation of what he meant by aristocracy was clear, but it was easily misconstrued. So, why not use some other term, perhaps "elites," a term we would use today? He did not have that option because the word was not used in America until the 1880s (Ryerson 2016, 483, footnote 4).

Adams's reading of history was that democracies often succumbed to the aristocratic quest for power. Democracies with a strong executive (the One) aligning with the Many were often able to resist aristocratic schemes. (But he also knew that, throughout history, the Monarch often colluded with the Aristocrats against the Many.) He thought the only chance for survival of the nascent United States republic was to have a strong executive. Based on this belief, he made a major political blunder as vice president.

As the new government was organizing, President Washington and the Senate struggled to find the best formal term to address the president. Adams used his position presiding in the Senate to advocate titles such as "His Most Benign Highness" and "His Majesty, the President." He feared that without such titles most Americans would devote their lives to private concerns and would not have enough incentive to serve as government leaders. How would the wily aristocrats be counter-balanced if government service were not made attractive (Ryerson 2016, 317–20)? Although Washington and the Senate agreed at first, the political tide turned against Adams. However, he continued to promote his ideas, resulting in the gag rule for vice presidents presiding over the Senate.

Adams's supposed advocacy of aristocracy was used mercilessly against him in the election of 1800. Jeffersonian leaders, themselves American aristocrats, cynically distorted Adams's ideas; they knew their campaign propaganda was not truthful. In 1805, Benjamin Rush, a friend of John Adams since the Continental Congress, wrote to him about a conversation with James Madison in which Madison stated he knew that Adams did not have "unfriendly designs" on the "form of our American governments" (Schutz and Adair 1966, 33). In other words, Jeffersonian-Republican leaders understood that Adams was not against democracy. Note that I have not accused Jefferson of spreading these lies. Presidential candidates at that time did not campaign; that dirty work was left to others. But it should be noted that Adams wrote to Jefferson, asking him to specify where in his writings he had advocated aristocracy (Thompson 1998, 269–75). Jefferson never responded.

Both the Jeffersonians and the Federalists feared that the opposition party would destroy American democracy. Jeffersonians mistakenly thought they preserved it with their victory. Neither party understood the danger Adams saw, so they did not inoculate our young democracy against aristocracy.

Given the heated rhetoric of his reelection campaign, peaceful transition from Federalists to Jeffersonians at the end of Adams's presidency was not guaranteed; that it happened helped solidify the legitimacy of the new system, the national community of the constitution. The thirteen states had been joined together in a stronger union.

Factionalism cost Adams reelection; six years later, in a letter to Benjamin Rush, Adams, in his inimitable style, states his hope that international trade would clarify the importance of community.

> Now commerce, the instrument of an universal alliance, establishing a channel of communication between man and man, from the North Pole to the South, renders it visible to the grossest eyesight that we are made for one another, that our destination is to be useful reciprocally, that we are members of the same body and children of the same family. (Schutz and Adair 1966, 71).

Adams's hopes were not realized; parties (factionalism) prevailed.

Insensitivity to the rise of aristocracy was only one factor undermining individuality within communities. Gradually, the equal right to life, liberty, and the pursuit of happiness was subverted by an emphasis on personal freedom. Several founders feared that, once independence was gained, the public spirit of the revolutionary era would be forgotten, as people pursued their own personal gain. Their fears were well-founded; individualism with little or no concern for the public good gradually took hold and was firmly implanted by the end of Andrew Jackson's presidency. The wide expanse of the new nation and the richness of its resources gave white men immense opportunities. Even though they benefitted greatly from government services, the myth that the nation developed because of rugged individualism became widely accepted.

THE MYTH OF RUGGED INDIVIDUALISM

Laura Ingalls Wilder's *Little House on the Prairie* books touted the rugged individualist as the lead character in settlement of the Great Plains. But Naomi Oreskes and Erik M. Conway argue that the stories were false, skipping details, such as the Ingalls family member who benefitted from the government-funded Iowa College for the Blind and the tuition provided for her attendance. This was not the only omission: "Throughout the stories, people of color are also expunged, leaving us with a dishonest story of 'white self-sufficiency' instead of an honest story of government-sponsored settlements whose costs were borne by native peoples" (Oreskes and Conway 2023, 184). And, as Heather Cox Richardson notes, "The real life of the Ingalls family was one in which the women and girls—not Pa—supported the family, and the West depended on the federal government" (Richardson 2023, 51).

The myth of rugged individualism conveniently ignores the large government role in establishing conditions that enabled personal success. As Jon Meacham points out, "The American ideal of what Henry Clay had called 'self-made men' in 1832 is so central to the national mythology that there's often a missing character in the story Americans like to tell about American prosperity: government which frequently helped create the conditions for the making of those men" (Meacham 2018, 180).

The list of government actions is long; in the decades after the peace treaty with Great Britain, there were significant government investments in the infrastructure needed for a thriving market economy. In the nineteenth century, governments invested in canals, highways, harbors, railroads, even banks. Political and military actions to secure more land (such as the Louisiana Purchase and conquest of large sections of Mexico, including, *inter alia,* what eventually became Texas and California), constitutional and other legal support for slavery, and after Reconstruction, a national government laissez-faire policy toward the South, plus restrictive legislation by state governments which enabled political-economic elites to impose the virtual slavery of sharecropping, enforced by Ku Klux Klan terrorism, are also on the list.

Individuals did not dig the Erie Canal, which gave farmers in the trans-Appalachia region a way to ship their produce to eastern markets. This stimulated settlement of Ohio and lands to the west. The myth of a continent with wide-open spaces led many to trek across the prairies to establish homesteads; but First Nations lived there. How could one person survive on a frontier already populated by Amerindians fighting for survival against the white race?

As Robert Putnam notes, both Frederick Jackson Turner's research and more "recent research suggest that the more enduring legacy of the frontier was individualism." In addition, he states, "Frontier life was indeed associated with a culture of boot-strap self-reliance and hostility to economic redistribution, an imprint still visible a century later" (Putnam 2020, 166). The reality is that Western settlement required supporting communities, including the wagon trains that crossed the prairies and the US cavalry that waged genocide against First Nations.

So contrary to common opinion, the West was not conquered by rugged individualists. Nevertheless, as Nancy Rosenblum points out, the myth overcame the reality of a large government (community) role, including railroads, land grants, and agricultural support. But many people "didn't acknowledge 'that the richest claim of all lay not in the minefields but in Washington.' This willful omission allows the settler to be turned into a pronounced ideology of nearly unfettered individualism, excepting only the voluntary assistance of people living nearby" (Rosenblum 2016, 53). The dominant image that remains is of a cowboy riding off alone into the sunset. Perception has eclipsed reality.

Individualism did not win the Civil War; huge armies were needed. And our president had, according to Carl Sandburg, an expansive definition of community, encompassing the globe: "Lincoln used the phrase, 'The Family of Man.' He saw the family as a unity. He hoped to see it move toward closer unity and wider freedom—everywhere" (Basler 1946, xx–xxi).

We the people won the Civil War, built the transcontinental railroads, and the Eisenhower Interstate Highway System a century later. Massive investments were also made in water and air transportation. These infrastructure projects were essential to improve the flow of commerce. Individualism did not protect the country from foreign threats; government did. All these are examples of public goods that increased the chances for hundreds of millions of people to thrive within multiple interrelated communities. Our nation was built by teamwork. It has been defended by teamwork. And we still depend on teamwork.

ADAMS AND SMITH: SHARED PRINCIPLES

Adams and Smith shared several principles applicable to the twenty-first century, principles that are also compatible with Christianity. That they agreed on some principles should not be a surprise, given Adams's appreciation for Smith's thought, perhaps most obvious in his use of extensive sections of *Theory of Moral Sentiments* in *Discourses on Davila* (Ryerson 2016, 504). He clearly agreed with Smith on the human desire for mankind's sympathy (Haraszti 1952, 170). Smith's sociability may have reinforced Adams's community orientation.

A scientific, evidence-based approach characterizes the work of both men. They were social scientists, not natural scientists; their work was based on extensive research and careful logic. Both were critical of ideological arguments. Smith criticized a spirit of system that valued theory above reality; Adams vociferously denounced factionalism. He wanted politics to be decided by carefully reasoned argument, not emotion and party spirit.

Smith, a valued adviser to the British government, was inclusive in his thought; he advocated using the best practices found anywhere in the world to solve problems. Adams changed from Massachusetts chauvinism to a surprising openness by the end of his life (Hill 2010).

Both emphasized the importance of education. While appreciating the potential of the division of labor to spread opulence to the lowest ranks of the people, Smith was concerned that the repetitive nature of modern industrial work would dumb down the working class so much that workers would be unable to fulfill their responsibilities as parents, citizens, and soldiers. Thus, he argued that government should be responsible for educating the working class. Adams also emphasized education, writing in *Thoughts on Government*: "LAWS for the liberal education of youth, especially of the lower class of people, are so extremely wise and useful, that to a humane and generous mind, no expense for this purpose would be thought extravagant" (Taylor 1979, IV 91). When he drafted the Massachusetts Constitution, Adams included a significant role for government in education; he was thrilled when that clause was included in the version ratified by the voters.

The abhorrence of irresponsibility, both individual and governmental, is clear in their writing. Smith was acerbic in his criticism of British government funding schemes for useless wars. He was similarly critical of irresponsibility on the part of the poor (for buying luxuries like tea and chocolate) and the wealthy (referring to silver and gold plate as "trifling superfluities"). Adams was critical of businessmen profiteering off the Revolutionary War; a responsible citizen should work for the common good, not strive for individual riches. In his letters from Europe, he repeatedly commented that the failure of states to meet their Confederation responsibilities made his diplomatic mission more difficult. Both Smith and Adams supported progressive taxes as just and responsible government policy.

And there is evidence that the principles they advocated would work. In the post–World War II period, the United States was a relatively egalitarian political economy. The GI Bill of Rights democratized higher education and expanded home ownership. There was bipartisan support for a massive infrastructure project (the Eisenhower Interstate Highway system). The Supreme Court's desegregation decision and bipartisan legislation attacked racial inequality. Taxes were progressive, providing resources for government programs. Economic gains from increased productivity were shared widely, so everyone benefited economically.

However, this ended in the 1970s; since then these gains have gone, predominantly, to the wealthy. In addition, the top income tax rates were radically reduced, making the income tax significantly less progressive. Tax cuts, along with CEO monopolization of productivity gains, radically increased the concentration of wealth. The top 1% of the population have steadily added to their income and wealth, while the other classes have stagnated, barely treading water.

CONCLUSION

The Founders' individuality within communities orientation has been forgotten. As John Adams feared two hundred years ago, when there is no public virtue, when faction prevails over the national interest, when venality is rampant, the essence of our society is lost, even though the form still exists (Schutz and Adair 1966, 119–20). This is not the democratic republic that Adams envisioned; we have fallen far short of the equal rights for all that our Founders promised. Adams's fears were misunderstood by his contemporaries. A very small group of elites now have immense economic and political power, demonstrating that his fears were well-founded. The aristocrats are economically and politically dominant; this has been aided by individualistic distortion of Christianity and by ignorance of the sociable, fair market Smith advocated.

The next chapters focus on benefits communities provide, especially the national community. Having written thus far of the three misinterpretations, it is now time to sketch out some of the benefits of sociability, time to argue that it would be worthwhile to correct the mistakes. These chapters are addressed especially to readers who are still dubious about individuality within communities. Market economies flourish when communities are strong because effective governments provide important services for everyone. And sociability increases happiness.

Chapter Five

Benefits of Sociability

Individuality in communities is an important implication of the thought of Smith and Adams and is crucial for Christianity, three sources of ideals for a good society. However, most economists focus on the free market and miss the sociability in Adam Smith's work. Liberty is emphasized at the expense of the equally important justice and equality elements in his simple secret for wealthy nations. Since the nineteenth century, distortion of his formula has contributed to immense increases in the wealth and power of the few at the expense of the many. Warnings of the dangers of "aristocracy," from our second President, misunderstood from the beginning, have been unheeded for centuries. The result is that individualistic elites dominate our politics and society at the expense of the common good. In addition, Christianity is too often given an individualistic meaning, ignoring the Great Commandment ("Love your neighbor as yourself"). But does it matter that we misinterpret them? This chapter moves on from these sources of political culture to examine the contributions of sociability to the general welfare.

Individualism has waxed and waned since the founding of this nation, but it has been excessive for the last half-century, resulting in a market economy that concentrates wealth and produces political power that twists democracy into plutocracy. This is democratic malpractice, manipulating politics to benefit a few, instead of promoting individuality within communities, the common good, the well-being of all. Current practice has enabled a small number of individualists to gain enormous wealth, while the middle and working classes are left behind.

When Democratic Party dominance of our political system ended in the mid-20th century, American capitalism was significantly affected. Nixon's "Southern strategy" turned the Republicans into the dominant party. Their "dog-whistle" racism, called "laissez-faire racism" by Robert Putnam (Putnam 2020, 241), gave them the power to enact market reforms that have moved the country from a more egalitarian market to an individualistic market. That market brought great wealth to a few resulting in an economic aristocracy and political power, which has paralyzed democracy. Often, when one party controls either the House, the Senate, or the presidency, and the other controls at least one of the three, our country has suffered because of unwillingness to legislate in a bipartisan fashion. The environment deteriorates, the globe simmers, racism festers, and education suffers, with little if any progress in providing equal educational opportunity for all young people. Class differences in health care remain; the Affordable Care Act (ACA) made a dent in this problem, but it is not universal, and partisanship has produced significant differences in coverage, depending on whether one lives in a red state or a blue state.

In the last half century, the middle-class and the poor have struggled economically, while the wealth of the 1 percent has increased obscenely, and the growth of the economy has slowed. Emmanuel Saez and Gabriel Zucman report that the top 0.1 percent have seen incomes increase by 320 percent. However, in that same period, working-class wages have had "an annual growth rate of 0.1%. . . . There is no evidence that the income of the rich has 'trickled down' to the working class. The working class has been shut off from economic growth" (Saez and Zucman 2019, 163–64). While income of the wealthy has increased eighty times as rapidly as stagnating workers' wages, three presidents have signed tax legislation that significantly reduced the highest rates. This is a stark contrast to Smith's suggestion of diffusing wealth to the lowest ranks of the people. Time will tell if workers' salary increases recently negotiated by unions change the long-term trend.

Does our political system promote justice when tax reductions enrich the wealthy and impoverish the government, making it difficult to finance crucial public services? Taxes are payments for government services, which the wealthy and corporations willingly receive. But do they pay their fair share? Where is the justice when the tax code results in billionaires having lower tax rates than the middle class? Is it fair that some wealthy corporations pay no taxes at all?

Politicians find that cutting taxes helps ensure reelection; however, people also like services, so large tax cuts have been made without reducing services. Of course, this results in more government debt and repeated increases in the federal debt ceiling. Tax reductions have privileged the wealthy, destroyed the American Dream, and broken an intergenerational compact. Edith Rasell provides numbers that support this statement:

> Nearly two-thirds of these tax cuts benefited the one-fifth of households with the highest incomes, and the top 1 percent received 22 percent; the one-fifth of households with the lowest incomes received just 3 percent of the cut. Tax cuts have contributed to the rise in inequality, the shortfall in government revenue and the increase in the federal debt. In 2018, some two-thirds of the national

debt was due to tax cuts and the unfunded wars fought since 9/11. (Rasell 2022, 174).

It took forty years (1942–1982) for the federal debt to reach $1 trillion; in the following forty-one years, it grew by more than $32 trillion. Tax cuts that further enriched the already wealthy were made without attention to the federal debt. The future of our grandchildren and great-grandchildren has been mortgaged; their dream will be a nightmare, unless there are massive changes in our priorities. This is not a plea for a Balanced Budget Amendment; it is a plea for a wise Keynesian approach—borrow to stimulate the economy in recessions and depressions, but repay the debt when the economy is sound—this crucial second part of Keynesian economics is usually ignored. And, yes, that means increased taxes for some Americans.

One reason for this unconscionable deferral of debt is lazy thinking about the source of government services. As consumers, we expect to pay for goods and services; some of this is financed by individual (personal) debt. Ultimately, we expect to repay loans; but this appears not to be the case with governmental borrowing. Unlike personal purchases, when we make income or property tax payments we do not immediately receive a product or a service, so we do not think of taxes as purchasing government services. Many politicians have used this difference to mislead Americans—sometimes labeling taxes as theft. The legislative habit of increasing benefits without raising revenue to pay for them adds to the deficit.

While it seems logical to balance the budget by reducing services, this is not politically feasible because of the popularity of the services, not to mention that many of the services are vitally necessary. Few, if any, people would advocate reducing the Defense Department's budget by a third or more. So what might be done to restore budget sanity? Politicians of all stripes need to remember Accounting 101: in addition to the expense side of the ledger, there is also an income side. Funding the IRS so that the tax code is fairly administered plus restoring graduated tax rates sufficient to pay current expenses in ordinary times would be fair and might even strengthen the economy.

Critics will argue, at this point, that higher taxes will kill the goose that lays the golden egg. History does not support this complaint. Saez and Zucman report that when highest tax rates were "quasi-confiscatory" in the United States after World War II, "growth was strong and widely shared" (Saez and Zucman 2019, 161). Thomas Piketty, analyzing data from around the world, argues that such high tax rates have been successful. "They have made it possible to greatly reduce the divergences of fortunes and incomes, while at the same time improving the situation of the middle and lower classes, developing the welfare state, and stimulating better economic and social performance overall" (Piketty 2022, 139).

Our Founders bequeathed us a dream, but greedy capitalists (forgetting that money is the means to produce goods and services, not an end in itself) and irresponsible taxation policies are destroying the dream by starving the government of the funds necessary to equalize opportunities for health care, education, and social services. To level the playing field, enhanced local, state, and national government action is needed. If a significant portion of increased tax revenues were allocated to needed government services and to retiring the federal debt, the generational injustice of bequeathing our great-grandchildren enormous debts would end. But justice for future generations cannot be at the expense of justice today; both current and future Americans deserve a government that responds to the promises of our Founders.

Can we argue that government insures domestic tranquility when shootings resulting in multiple deaths occur, on average, more than once a day? Can we argue that our governments are securing for us the blessings of liberty when climate change imperils the world and when millions are unemployed (or underemployed) because of automation and globalization? These failures appear to be violations of the oath to support the Constitution that all state legislators and members of Congress must swear in order to take office.

One Representative made a suggestion that would have helped, but predictably it has not been taken up by Congress. In his last term in office, Joe Kennedy, III called for "moral capitalism." The religious implications of this term are obvious and consistent with arguments of Christian scholars. In addition to arguments in a preceding chapter, note Russell Pregeant's statement that laissez-faire individualism is "idolatrous from a biblical perspective . . . it clearly exalts the human will above the commandments of God" (Pregeant 2016, 180; see also 126). There is solid Biblical grounding for Kennedy's proposal.

In addition, his call has a solid economic basis of which he seemed unaware. Centuries before Kennedy's speech, Adam Smith advocated capitalism with justice and equal opportunity. A long list of Smith scholars emphasize that he advocated ethical capitalism, not laissez-faire (See Hill 2016, Chapters 1–3, for detailed support of this point). Both parties could atone for their democratic malpractice by adopting Smith's approach: ethical capitalism for all the people. This, however, would require a major shift in the current American ideology of excessive individualism, emphasizing instead the more inclusive idea of teamwork, in short, individuality within communities.

This is not a recipe for stifling conformity nor an attack on individuality. It is, instead, a call for a less simplistic way of thinking; we are not limited to either individuality or community. Life is more complex and better when individuality is embedded in communities. The dichotomies listed in Chapter 1 give multiple examples of this more complex thinking.

Two points must be clarified: (1) individualism is economically counterproductive; and (2) capitalism thrives because of significant community contributions.

COUNTERPRODUCTIVE INDIVIDUALISM

Business requires multiple interconnected communities; individualism in business is counterproductive. This is not an attack on businesspeople; capitalism is a powerful way to organize economies, and many capitalists are ethical people. Here is the perspective of a retired banker:

> The capitalists I have known (businessmen, entrepreneurs, manufacturers, to name a few) are hard-working, honest, diligent people. These are the ones who dream up opportunities, start businesses, hire people, dedicate their lives to long hard work without certainty of success. They provide jobs, advancement, benefits, and family care without regard to sexual, racial, or social differences. In my world, these are the people who provide opportunity, hope, and prosperity for the largest group of people in the nation. (email, January 27, 2017).

One can reasonably assume that most businesspeople are moral participants in market economies, models of the ethical capitalism Smith advocated and exemplified by people that retired banker had worked with. Nonetheless, there is a lethal virus in the system. Main Street capitalism, witnessed by that banker, producing goods and services, is not the capitalism practiced on Wall Street, which instead focuses on profit at all costs, profit through financial manipulation, profit without regard to harm done to stakeholders.

As Edith Rasell states, the primary purpose of the financial industry (banking, investment, insurance, and real estate) is to "take the savings of households and corporations and channel them into productive uses. But instead of serving the needs of the real economy, the deregulated financial sector is now much more focused on quickly making money from money, through short-term, speculative, and often risky activities" (Rasell 2022, 155). Wall Street has forgotten its purpose, raising capital to enable production; it focuses instead on the metric for evaluating success (profit).

Main Street capitalism has been supplanted by Wall Street capitalism as the dominant form of capitalism in the United States. Our economy has transitioned from profiting by productivity (Main Street) to profiting by financial maneuvers (Wall Street). Finance capitalism has transformed Wall Street into a casino; its sole purpose is maximizing shareholder value, by any and all means, regardless of the number of viable companies destroyed, the number of factories shuttered, the number of jobs exported to other countries. Anna Bernasek made this point a decade ago:

> The whole vast and intricate financial universe, with all its sober rules and gray-haired regulators, had been diabolically converted by the nation's brightest minds into a casino where gamblers were risking mountainous piles of other people's money. Before the chips fell, those gamblers claimed a lion's share of false winnings and absconded with fortunes intact, leaving behind a generation's worth of toxic residue for the eventual contemplation of investing clients and the taxpaying public. (Bernasek 2010, 6–7).

Commenting on the mortgage crisis of 2008, Joseph Stiglitz writes that banks "became gambling casinos—gambling with other people's money, knowing that the taxpayer would step in if the losses were too great" (Stiglitz 2015, 63). When their risks failed, the bankers were rescued by the community, in the form of the federal government, which spent billions of dollars to rescue them—socialism for the rich.

This is a modern form of usury, resulting in excessive profits, which made the financiers billionaires at great cost to everyone else. For centuries, usury was seen as a major sin; people looked down on money-lenders. Good people did not earn money from money; governments passed laws banning usury. Religious and legal prohibitions long constrained capital markets. However, modern capital markets have no compunction about usury; they practice it on a colossal scale, at the expense of the economy, democracy, and equal opportunity.

It is no longer enough to finance corporations as long-term investments. Producing more goods or introducing new products or services was once the primary goal; market success for the corporation then resulted in profits, leading to increased stock values and dividends. Profits were a metric for determining how well the corporation fulfilled its function, not the goal itself.

There is confusion about means and ends. Production is no longer the purpose; profits accumulate too slowly that old-fashioned way. Now profits are the goal. Rapid turnover of stocks, aided by sophisticated computer programs, produces quick gains for some investors, but little if any benefit for the corporations. How many viable companies have disappeared because of this form of greed? This seems very short-sighted; as Paul Knowlton and Aaron Hedges point out, "Value that is not sustained is also not maximized" (Knowlton and Hedges 2021, 113; see also 32–4). Some financiers—modern-day pirates—buy viable companies and sell the component parts for enormous profits, even though these companies could have provided larger benefits, spread over a longer time, for many stakeholders. Individualism of many financiers has led them to ignore the long-term interests of stakeholders in favor of short-term profits for shareholders.

Advocates of shareholder value do not care that they could do well enough while doing great good for millions of workers, consumers, and the towns and cities where their facilities are located. They probably do not know (or care) that doing good in this way would follow Smith's model for a market with justice, liberty, and equality. For Smith, capital was a means of producing goods or services, with good wages for workers. Profits resulting from success were to be reinvested, not wasted on conspicuous consumption. But in the last half-century, capitalism in the United States has shifted from stakeholder to shareholder capitalism, from profiting by producing goods to profiting through financial maneuvers.

Wall Street is not the only villain. The pharmaceutical sector has long made excess profits because it is able to avoid the supply and demand discipline of the market. This is a hotly debated subject, but a 2000–2018 study analyzing profits of 35 pharmaceutical companies and 357 nonpharmaceutical companies, found a statistically significant difference in profit margins: "The median net income (earnings) expressed as a fraction of revenue was significantly greater for pharmaceutical companies compared with non-pharmaceutical companies (13.8% vs 7.7%)" (Ledley 2020, 834).

Obviously, the world owes pharmaceutical corporations a debt of gratitude for the rapid development of vaccines that tamed the COVID 19 virus. But we should not forget that huge government subsidies financed much of that spectacular scientific and manufacturing miracle. The great good it did and that drugs have done in other cases, such as virtually eliminating polio from the world, deserve praise. But there are too many cases of price gouging. For instance, the *Boston Sunday Globe*, March 1, 2020, reported on the cost of insulin; price gouging was bankrupting diabetics and killing them (because they either could not afford the medication or they rationed it, which led to complications and death).

The pharmaceuticals industry has not been shy about using its political muscle to avoid market controls on the costs of its medicines. In 2003, it successfully lobbied for legislation that prevented Medicare from negotiating prices for bulk purchases of drugs, privileging company profits over the health of individuals (see Hill 2016, 134). Congressmen were for sale, and Pharma was buying—it takes two to tango. One assumes that constituents of the bought Congressmen were not invited to the dance and were not aware of their representatives' dereliction of duty.

Neoliberal shareholder capitalism has produced a plethora of billionaires. Executive compensation is far more than the yardstick J. P. Morgan suggested a century ago; he argued that anything above a 20:1 ratio would be dangerous for a corporation. Fifty years ago, the ratio was 40:1. More recently, the ratio has become obscene; Sarah Anderson and Sam Pizzigati examined compensation at the three hundred firms with the lowest median wages in 2020. They found that the CEO-worker pay gap grew from 604:1 in 2020 to 670:1 in 2021, with forty-nine of the firms having ratios greater than 1,000:1, including all workers, throughout the world (Anderson and Pizzigati 2022, 1). If one eliminates workers in other countries, the contrast is less stark but still appalling. Lawrence Mishel and Jori Kandra found that in 2020 in the United States, CEO pay was 351 times that of a typical worker; that was an increase of more than 1,300 percent since 1978, a period when the stock market grew by 817 percent (Mishel and Kandra 2021, 1). CEOs had an average increase of 31 percent per year while workers' wages were basically unchanged. It strains credulity to argue that such raises are a reward for increased productivity. Mishel and Kandra's statistics demonstrate this. "The 1,322.2% growth in realized CEO compensation from 1978 . . . to 2020 far exceeded the growth in productivity, profits, or stock market values in that period" (Mishel and Kandra 2021, 9–10). A more likely explanation is that CEOs simply have significantly more political power than do workers, both within their corporations and at all levels of our government.

Another way to illustrate the impoverishment of America's working classes is to look at shares of national income. Mishel and Kandra found that, between 1978 and 2020, "Most of the rise of inequality took the form of redistributing wages from the bottom 90%—whose share of wages fell from 69.8% to 60.9%—to the top 1.0%—whose wage share nearly doubled, rising from 7.3% to 13.2%, with most of the increase accruing to the top 0.1%, whose share of all wages grew from 1.6% to 5.0%" (Mishel and Kandra 2021, 16).

Thomas Piketty argues that CEO power has increased since the 1980s: "The evidence suggests that executives began to devote considerable effort to persuading others that enormous raises were warranted, which was not always difficult to do, since it is hard to measure how much any individual executive contributes to the firm's success. What is more, compensation committees were often constituted in a rather incestuous fashion" (Piketty 2020, 533). He also writes that it is hard "to find any statistically significant correlation between executive pay and firm performance (or productivity)" (Piketty 2020, 533). And, in a more recent work, he continues to argue that "there is no meaningful relation between managers' salaries and their economic performance." In addition, their pay has "mainly negative effects on low and middle-level salaries" (Piketty 2022, 138–39). Additional evidence that such outlandish salaries are not based on superior results in the stock market and with profits for the corporation is provided by Timothy Noah who notes that "One survey 'compared the 25 highest-earning S&P CEOs to the 25 highest-earning S&P companies' and there was only one match" (Noah 2022).

Individualism on this colossal scale seems to be a contradiction to Friedman's emphasis on maximizing shareholder value. Some shareholders—CEOs—benefit; but their gains are at the expense of other shareholders because their compensation packages often include significant stock options. Moreover, their compensation is often based on the internal politics of the corporation, not measurable contributions to its value. Mishel and Kandra argue that CEOs gain such high salaries "not by virtue of their contribution to economic output but by virtue of their position of power. . . . CEO compensation could be reduced across the board and the economy would not suffer any loss of output" (Mishel and Kandra 2021, 16).

But CEO control over corporate boards and executive compensation panels means that obscene salaries, having no relation to value produced for the corporation, are common. This is clearly a conflict of interest. As Robert Putnam states, corporate titans' "ideology of individualism . . . barely masks selfishness and an air of superiority" (Putnam 2020, 5). Meanwhile, many hard-working middle and working class people struggle. This is not the market with justice, liberty, and equality that Adam Smith envisioned.

CEOs are not the only villains of this story; Heather Boushey argues that the pseudoscience known as supply-side economics "created perfect conditions for income and wealth inequality to grow and thrive, crimping economic mobility to the detriment of us all" (Boushey 2019, xiii).

Such large differences in earnings affect the economy and society in multiple ways. George DeMartino argues that "Inequality harms everyone, not just those who face deprivation. Everyone in unequal societies suffers from the risks of violence—though the risk is certainly not born equally—such that even the well-to-do feel deeply insecure and must take steps to protect themselves from physical and other threats. Everyone suffers from the erosion of fraternity and community institutions" (DeMartino 2022, 59). Jesse Norman notes that there is a "growing body of evidence that extreme or entrenched inequality is not only morally indefensible but harms educational and job opportunities, reduces economic growth and undermines social trust" (Norman 2018, 240–41).

Thomas Piketty agrees: "Historical experience shows, moreover, that such immense inequalities of wealth have little to do with the entrepreneurial spirit and are of no use in promoting growth" (Piketty 2014, 572–73). More evidence comes from Europe, where Piketty found that smaller raises did not reduce productivity: "Specifically, in the 1980s and 1990s, executives in German, Swedish, and Danish firms had to make do with far less fabulous raises than their English and US counterparts, yet this did not harm their firms' productivity or competitiveness—quite the contrary" (Piketty 2020,

499). Lawrence Mishel and Jori Kandra reached a similar conclusion for the United States: if top executives "*were paid less there would be no loss of productivity or output in the economy*" (Mishel and Kandra 2021, 12 [italics in the original]).

Such outlandish salaries have not made United States corporations more competitive. Thomas Philippon found that "Competition has declined in most sectors of the US economy" and that "lack of competition leads to lower wages, investment, productivity, growth, and more inequality" (Philippon 2019, 9–10). He also "was surprised by the strength of the evidence in favor of competition," which "lowers prices and increases real wages and standards of living." In addition, it "is good for investment," innovation, and productivity (Philippon 2019, 288). Correlation is, of course, not causation, but one would expect such outlandish salaries to come with improved results, instead of the declines noted by Philippon.

Heather Boushey's meta-study of inequality confirms that "income inequality obstructs the process of becoming an innovator—and thus, constrains innovation itself" (Boushey 2019, 62). She also found evidence that inequality led to "fewer startups, which in turn could be a factor behind the slowdown in US productivity" (Boushey 2019, 134). That can impede economic growth. In addition, she notes that inequality "gives the wealthy the power in the political realm to lobby successfully for low taxes, regulatory changes in their favor, and out-sized electoral influence" (Boushey 2019, 192).

Joseph Stiglitz points out the impact of inequality on crucial "public goods, such as infrastructure, technology, and education, which contribute to long-term economic prosperity and growth." He argues that reducing economic disparities, in contrast, "has clear economic as well as social benefits" (Stiglitz 2015, 288). He also writes that "mainstream studies" have repeatedly demonstrated that inequality reduces economic growth; "Even the International Monetary Fund, not known for its radical economic stances, has come to recognize the adverse effects of inequality on economic performance" (Stiglitz 2015, 420). Further, he states that "Societies with fewer economic disparities perform better" for everyone (Stiglitz 2015, 323)."

Inequality bodes ill for the future, as it tends to reduce investment in necessary societal goods and services. Proliferation of the mega-wealthy weakens the economy. It reduces demand because "the marginal propensity to consume is lower at higher wealth quintiles" (Fisher 2019, 1). Josh Bivens agrees that this reduced demand will "constrain American economic growth in coming years" (Bivens 2017, 1–2). If the working and middle classes had higher earnings, they would spend a higher proportion of those additional earnings. The result would be that "aggregate consumption would be higher with a transfer from high-wealth households to low-wealth households" (Fisher 2019, 19). Bivens points out: "boosting wages of the bottom 90 percent would not just raise *these* households' incomes and welfare . . . it would also boost overall growth" (Bivens 2017, 3–4).

John Campbell and John Hall argue that economic growth is reduced by inequality and insufficient social cohesion. "Government investment in infrastructure, education, health, and public goods necessary to sustain economic growth can suffer. This stands in obvious contrast to the emphasis on human capital as the source of progress that lies at the heart of the work of Adam Smith" (Campbell and Hall 2021, 123).

IMF researchers confirm that high levels of inequality reduce growth:

> Although the relation between inequality and growth can be complex, higher levels of inequality are associated, on average, with lower and less durable growth. Hence, even from the perspective of the goal of fostering growth, attention to inequality is necessary. Moreover, high levels of inequality may lead to latent social conflicts that ultimately translate into political backlash against the pursuit of free market policies, including globalization. (Ostry 2019, 107).

The same researchers found that "the things that governments have typically done to redistribute do not seem to have led to bad growth outcomes unless they were extreme. And the resulting narrowing of inequality helped support faster and more durable growth" (Ostry 2019, 105; see also Ostry 2014).

Greater economic equality is good for growth. The nation would be stronger economically if there were not such a sharp socioeconomic class divide. Remove the chasm that separates the upper class from the rest, and there would still be an upper class, but a more equitable wage structure would result in a stronger economy.

Market individualism is also counterproductive for the economy in other ways, as the 2008 economic crisis demonstrates. Many Americans suffered because of corporate malfeasance, but the government rescued "Too Big to Fail" corporations. Alternatively, had the government been more active in restraining market excesses, the economy would have been healthier. Andres Solimano has argued that "Historically, the frequency of financial crises has been higher in periods of liberal and neoliberal capitalism than in times of regulated capitalism" (Solimano 2014, 85). Solimano points out that, while Marx, Schumpeter, Keynes and other great economists understood that capitalism could be very productive, they also knew that it has self-destructive tendencies such as causing financial crises, unemployment, income inequality, and damage to the environment (Solimano 2014, 110). He notes that financial elites vigorously protect their independence during boom phases, but are quick to use their political influence to gain massive rescue packages at the nadir of economic cycles. Such welfare for the rich does not reduce their support for austerity policies that make "the working and middle classes pay for their excesses. And yet the financial sector blames the welfare state for the crisis" (Solimano 2014, 109).

He is not alone in spelling out the negative impact of austerity policies. IMF researchers point out that austerity policies have multiple harmful effects: increases in unemployment and inequality, and "declines in wage income and in the wage share of income, and increases in long-term unemployment" (Ostry 2019, 71 and 77).

That economic inequality is quite significant in the United States should not surprise anyone. According to Credit Suisse, from 2015 to 2020, the top 1 percent of the population in the United States controlled 35 percent of the wealth; that inequality is even more severe in other countries is only cold comfort (Shorrocks 2020, 38). The Gini Index, a measure of economic inequality, had the United States ratio in 2019 at 0.41, much more equal than South Africa at 0.63 but less equal than dozens of other countries, such as the Slovak Republic at 0.23 (in 2019), Czech Republic at 0.25 (2019), Norway at 0.28 (2019), and Germany at 0.32 (2018). This ratio puts us behind most of our NATO allies, and even behind Russia (World Bank).

Considering the entire world, 1 percent of the population—millionaires and billionaires—control 43.4 percent of wealth (Shorrocks 2020, 29). Alissa Quart argues that the wealth inequality gap has significant consequences: "when the top 1 per cent has so much—so much more than even the top 5 or 10 per cent—the middle class is financially and also mentally outclassed at each step" (Quart 2018, 6–7).

Stiglitz argues that the causes of growing inequality, such as monopolies and preferential tax treatment "undermine the efficiency of the economy" (Stiglitz 2015, 89–90). Rebalancing will be better for all. Multiple studies have demonstrated that more equal nations have stronger economies, stay out of recessions longer, recover from recessions more rapidly, have better health outcomes (in all classes), and score higher on happiness rankings (Hill 2016, 87–9).

The negative consequences of market individualism include poorer health for many Americans and increased social pathologies (Hill 2016, 87–9). One could argue that recent declines in United States life expectancy are due to penurious welfare policies. Indeed Jason Beckfield and Clare Bambra have estimated "that life expectancy in the US would be approximately 3.77 years longer, if it had just the average social policy generosity of the other 17 OECD nations" (Beckfield and Bamba 2016, 30). In addition, a macro-history trend should be noted; when Great Powers change their economic emphasis from production to finance, international power declines (Phillips 2002, 172–74ff). Financialization of the economy may be undermining United States power in the world.

The wealthy withdraw from society into their exclusive enclaves. They care for their children, sometimes with criminal acts to secure admission to preferred schools (landing several in federal prison). They apply political pressure to reduce taxes and to underfund the IRS, making it difficult for government to enforce the tax code. Underfunding the IRS severely retards the government's ability to collect taxes to reduce the federal debt. Many wealthy people practice tax avoidance, made easier by their success lobbying for loopholes. One analysis of IRS data found that, between 2014 and 2018, the richest twenty-five Americans paid 3.4 percent in taxes on $401 billion in increased worth, in contrast to 14 percent in federal taxes (on $70,000 in earnings) for the median American household (Eisenger 2021). Their pressure is effective because politicians are well aware of who pays for election campaigns.

Their political success "starves the beast," making it impossible for government to increase opportunities for the poor and middle class unless it resorts to deficit spending and thus adds to the federal debt. Starving the beast is pernicious and extremely costly; Putnam has pointed out the impact of such policies. He cites three studies calculating the societal costs of unequal opportunity; using different methods, the studies reached "broadly comparable—and surprisingly large—estimates." For instance, a 2012 study calculated a "staggering" societal burden of $4.75 trillion (Putnam 2015, 231–33).

Over 250 years ago, commenting on the British constitution, John Adams inveighed against selfishness similar to what this chapter presents:

> The constitution is not grounded on "the enormous faith of millions made for one." It stands not on the supposition that kings are the favourites of heaven; that their power is more divine than the power of the people, and unlimited but by their own will and discretion. It is not built on the doctrine that a few nobles or rich commons have a right to inherit the earth, and all the blessings and pleasures of it: and that the multitude, the million, the populace, the vulgar, the mob, the herd and the rabble, as the great always delight to call them, have no rights at all, and were made only for their use, to be robbed and butchered at their pleasure. No, it stands upon this principle, that the meanest and lowest of the people, are, by the unalterable indefeasible laws of God and nature, as well entitled to the benefit of the air to breathe, light to see, food to eat, and clothes to wear, as the nobles or the king. All men are born equal: and the drift of the British constitution is to preserve as much of this equality, as is compatible with the people's security against foreign invasions and domestic usurpation. (Taylor I, 1977, 167–68).

The Founders of this country did not intend to replace British monarchy with an aristocracy of wealth. But their ideals have been subverted; we are now back to where we started. While we do not have a monarch, we do have economic and political dominance by wealthy elites.

The egalitarian conclusion to Adams's letter brings us to an important argument for greater sociability; the elite receive enormous benefits from community, worth much more than the benefits the lower and middle classes receive. These benefits are almost never acknowledged. Let us now examine community contributions that facilitate capitalist enterprise.

COMMUNITY CONTRIBUTIONS TO CAPITALISM

Wealth is not produced by individuals but, as James Truslow Adams put it, is a "social product" (Adams 1932, 410). Capitalism simply cannot thrive based on rugged individualism; the community, in the form of governments at the federal, state, and local levels, provides numerous essential services. This is not simply my opinion; Francis Fukuyama argues "that social capital has a significant impact on the vitality and scale of economic organizations" (Fukuyama 1995, 101). Laws (such as those governing contracts and incorporation) make it possible for strangers to work together, but sociability makes such interactions more efficient (Fukuyama 1995, 150). The laws Fukuyama references are, in a democracy, sociable products.

Social capital includes much more than government, but let us concentrate there. Most people never think of the wide range of services provided by government. For instance, how many people ever give a thought to infrastructure? Surely highways and airports are valuable to everyone, but are especially valuable for commerce.

Jet passenger planes provide a good example; the technology was developed for the military. Boeing learned how to make safe jets, such as the 707, by building the KC-135 refueling planes for the Strategic Air Command. This was an extremely important lesson, one the British did not learn until their Comet, the first commercial jet airliner, developed metal fatigue and fell apart in mid-air. In addition, the FAA certifies the air-worthiness of passenger airplanes. How many people would fly on any new plane without some safety certification process? Most airports are built and operated by government entities. And the planes take off and land safely because air-traffic controllers—government employees—are on duty.

Aircraft technology is only one way that government aids the economy. The following items are not intended as a complete list of such services; they are examples of the range of benefits people in the United States, including those artificial individuals known as corporations, receive from government. The categories are organized following the preamble to the Constitution.

"We the people of the United States, in order to . . .

form a more perfect union

A major reason for abandoning the Articles of Confederation was that having thirteen states with different economic policies impeded commerce. The powers granted to the states made them virtually independent countries. Such disunion meant they were unable to agree on repaying Revolutionary War debts, which resulted in severe constraints on trade with Europe. But once the new Constitution was implemented, trade with Europe was revitalized.

The Constitution also provided a domestic benefit for business by establishing a large free-trade zone along the Atlantic coast from Maine to Georgia. This expanded enormously as the United States opened territory beyond the Appalachian Mountains, bought Louisiana, and conquered and otherwise obtained land stretching to the Pacific coast and beyond. American businesses benefited from this enormous free trade zone for well over a century before Europe achieved similar gains by establishing the Common Market, now expanded to the European Union. Imagine how difficult all interstate commerce would be if there were import duties at state boundaries throughout the continent. Of course, economic regulations today are not perfectly uniform throughout the United States; California and other states, for instance, have more stringent auto emissions standards. But on the whole, freedom of interstate commerce, which did not exist under the Articles of Confederation, has been a gold mine for American companies, a gold mine that is not noticed because it is part of the assumed environment.

There is potential for more benefits from a more perfect union, but that would require tax fairness. Because many wealthy people do not pay a fair share, the government is starved of funds that would promote equal opportunity, which is part of my definition of a more perfect union. (Remember that one of the reasons for the Constitutional Convention was the failure of some states to pay a fair share of the Revolutionary War debt—i.e., a fair share of taxes.)

Establish Justice

Administration of justice: both civil and criminal courts provide important benefits for individuals and corporations. Unbiased adjudication of the law establishes an environment in which businesses and entrepreneurs can flourish.

SEC and transparency in capital markets: this agency's oversight makes it possible for investors to trust the market; as a result, Wall Street is a powerful capital-raising behemoth. However, contemporary casino capitalism may destroy that trust for many investors.

Patent and copyright laws

Insure Domestic Tranquility . . .

Police

Courts

Fire departments

EMTs (some are government employees)

TSA

While none of these is perfect, one shudders to imagine life without them. The economic benefits of these services are enormous.

Provide for the Common Defense . . .

International security

Economic stimulus (but note that non-defense spending is more productive, providing more stimulus than defense spending)

Creation of mass manufacturing: the impetus behind modern industrial technology was the development of machine tools to make standardized parts for military weapons. (Oreskes and Conway 2023, 123–24).

State Department: diplomacy to establish and maintain peaceful relations with other countries, therefore reducing the need for military action. This should be the first option in international affairs, but in recent decades it has been supplanted by the military.

Promote the General Welfare . . .

Incorporation (Inc., LLC): statute law established limited liability. Before such laws were passed, financing new commercial and industrial projects had been difficult because liability was unlimited; incorporation laws unleashed capitalism. However, it is such old news that we forget how important it is. This is the *sine qua non* of market economies; the mind boggles at its value for investors. The wealthy are overwhelmingly the main beneficiaries.

Public schools: an educated work-force is of immense value to the economic system. Economic historians know that education stimulates economic growth (see Hill 2016, 148–49). Expansion of educational opportunities through the GI

Bill of Rights was an important reason that the post-war boom was stronger and lasted longer than historians thought it would;

Financial aid for college and university students

Consumer product safety laws: for example, milk has been safe for many decades (after a long history of problems) because of government standards established in collaboration with dairy farmers.

Courts: protecting contractual and property rights, among other benefits.

Affordable Care Act

CDC

EPA

NSF

OSHA

Consular services: the Department of State, with commercial attachés in embassies around the world, supports American businesses involved in international trade.

Passports

Money: producing currency as well as maintaining its stability. The hyper-inflation in Germany after World War I is an example of how important this is.

Banking: the government's role in regulating banks (and stabilizing them in financial crises) facilitates commerce. Stiglitz found that IMF assistance to banks (bank bailouts) was at or near the top of a variety of lists of corporate welfare (including lists from conservative think tanks) (Stiglitz 2010, 388).

Leasing government land for resource extraction, such as coal companies that have leases "virtually for free" (Stiglitz 2010, 199–200).

Support for medical and scientific research (on the importance of the government role in science and technology, see Sachs 2008, 220–21).

Public-private partnerships developed important technologies such as railroads, electricity, telephone systems, radio, aviation, television, digital computing, microwave technology (see Oreskes and Conway 2023, 403).

Social Security

Tax benefits for IRAs and 401(k) plans (the benefits of these go disproportionately to the wealthy)

Parks and playgrounds: national, state and local governments develop and maintain these. Urban tree cover (often planted and maintained by city parks departments) reduces heat islands and thus provides some natural air-conditioning, to say nothing about psychological benefits, such as increased happiness.

Public works, such as garbage collection, water, sewer systems, snow removal

Flood control systems

Hydro-electric dams (TVA, for example, provides both electricity and flood control benefits)

Commuter transportation systems (e.g., subways)

Eisenhower Interstate Highway system (and other roads and highways)

Port facilities

Airports and air traffic controllers

And secure the blessings of liberty to ourselves and our posterity, do ordain and establish this Constitution for the United States of America."

All of us, corporations and the wealthy included, receive enormous benefits from government services. Just who is that mythical, undeserving welfare queen driving around in her Cadillac? Perhaps occupants of chauffeured limousines are the real welfare beneficiaries.

This is not to deny that welfare programs have sometimes been abused, that some welfare recipients seem to live very well while hard-working poor people, not on welfare, struggle (Vance 2016, 138–49). It is easy to spread propaganda about programs that provide direct payments to poor people; however, the less obvious but much larger benefits the wealthy receive from government services are rarely subjected to political attack.

Ronald Reagan's famous campaign canard against welfare was consistent with much economic thinking at that time. Amartya Sen wrote from a somewhat different perspective:

> In many economic models, private goods are the only ones around, and this is typically the case when the "invisible hand" is given the task of doing visible

> good. But in fact, public goods are important in most economies and cover a wide range of services from roads and street lighting to defense. There is much evidence that the share of public goods in national consumption has grown rather dramatically in most countries in the world. (Sen 1977, 330).

The multiplicity of contributions by government to market economies is not a recent discovery. Adam Smith wrote about multiple government contributions. Giovanni Arrighi, quoting Donald Winch, points out Smith's clear understanding that a strong state was necessary to establish "the conditions for the existence of the market." And he lists many "spheres in which Smith advised the legislator to intervene":

> the provision of protection from internal and external threats to the security of individuals and the state (police and national defense), the administration of justice, the provision of the physical infrastructure needed to facilitate trade and communication, the regulation of money and credit, and the education of the mass of the population to counter the negative effects of the division of labor on its intellectual qualities. (Arrighi 2007, 42–3).

The services listed above are public goods that benefit everyone, but the wealthy benefit more. What is the basis of that statement? Try this thought experiment. What is the dollar value of streets and highways for Ms. Average American? Driving to the supermarket or a movie or commuting to work obviously has value, but is that value about the same, a little bit less, or a lot less than the dollar value of streets and highways for Mr. Daddy Warbucks? He depends on government for many things, such as infrastructure, to transport raw materials, to enable employees to get to work, to deliver goods and services. We all benefit from government services, but it seems patently obvious that the wealthy benefit significantly more. This is most obvious in the benefits coming from incorporation (limited liability) laws.

Without statutes of incorporation the modern stock market could not exist. The economy would be much smaller than it is today because many projects would never get off the ground for fear that one could lose all one's assets, not just the capital invested in the project. To get an approximation of the government's contribution requires totaling the market value of all stocks listed on United States stock exchanges. The Dow Jones and other stock indices do not provide this figure; they are compilations of individual share prices for a selected group of corporations. To get this total one must multiply all the outstanding shares for each listed corporation by their market price.

The actual amount is mind-boggling: according to the World Bank, total market value of listed domestic companies in the United States in 2018 was $30,436,313.05 million (World Bank 2021). A more recent source had a much larger number. "The total market capitalization of the US stock market is $50,808,508.7 million (12/31/2020). The market value is the total market cap of all U.S. based public companies listed in New York Stock Exchange, Nasdaq Stock Market or OTCQX U.S. Market" (Siblis 2021). Yes, you read that correctly; that is $50 million million. Whichever figure is more accurate, the total is virtually incomprehensible.

Legislation enabling incorporation was one part of government action that provided a foundation for capitalism. Robert Bellah argues that such legislation had a now-forgotten *quid pro quo*: incorporation was "a concession of public authority to a private group in return for service to the public good, with effective public accountability" (Bellah 1985, 290). In addition, Francis Fukuyama states that government legislation created "a stable system of property rights," the critical step enabling industrialization (Fukuyama 1995, 63). Government services, such as laws governing contracts and commerce, reinforce the conclusion that Mr. Daddy Warbucks receives immense unacknowledged government benefits, with a dollar value far more than the benefits Ms. Average American receives. The difference is astronomical.

Given the immense value that incorporation statutes created, a reasonable person would assume that there would be some recognition of this benefit provided by the government. This has not been the case. For decades, the biggest United States corporations have been successful at avoiding taxes; in 2020, fifty-five of the largest paid no corporate taxes, receiving $3.5 billion in tax rebates instead (Gardner and Wamhoff 2021).

Income tax deductions provide another type of government benefit. Bill McKibben reports that "The total value of all the real estate in the United States is $33.6 trillion" (McKibben 2022, 151). The mortgage interest deduction from federal income taxes is a significant benefit for those with enough resources to invest in real estate. Similarly, tax benefits for college savings plans and government support for retirement plans, such as IRAs, are significant contributions to wealthier individuals because, in contrast to ordinary workers, they can afford to defer some income during their earning years in order to save for the future.

Such government support means that the United States devotes a larger proportion of its economy to social benefits than does Sweden (Hacker 2016, 778). That point deserves emphasis; social welfare is a larger share of the United States economy than in Sweden! But people are unaware of the government's largesse because much of it comes as exclusions from taxable income, not direct payments.

Since the wealthy receive more in government services, progressive taxation is fair. This opinion is based on the taxation principles of the father of capitalism. Adam Smith's first principle was that subjects should "contribute towards the support of the government . . . in proportion to the revenue which they respectively enjoy under the protection of the state" (Smith 1791, III

255–56). In addition to arguing for a higher taxation rate for the wealthy, Smith supported luxury taxes (Smith 1791, III 96 and 284). In short, because the wealthy derive more benefit from government services than the other classes, more progressive taxes should be enacted to make taxation commensurate with benefits received.

Higher tax rates for the wealthy would have societal benefits. Governments could reduce national debt and/or provide more services that would be good for the economy, for example, education through the university level. Piketty argues that equality and education make economic development possible, "not the veneration of property, stability and inequality" (Piketty 2022, 139). He is not alone in valuing education highly; David Warsh writes of the importance of education for increasing knowledge, "the engine of economic growth" (Warsh 2006, 342). Education is a major factor stimulating the economy.

CONCLUSION

How should this be done? Would restoration of higher income tax rates (perhaps going back to the rates before the Bush tax cuts) be a better approach than a wealth tax? What about a significant estate tax? I am not qualified to make a recommendation, but I will make a prediction. Any proposal to increase taxes on the wealthy will produce an outcry of class warfare. But is it class warfare or a plea for fairness? Too many people forget the purpose of taxes—payment for services rendered. Given that the wealthy receive significantly greater benefits from government, and given the support of Adam Smith for progressive taxation, it seems that higher effective taxes on the wealthy would be fair, especially since many wealthy people pay a lower effective rate than the median American taxpayer. And it is especially unfair to foist bills for services we are receiving now on future generations through the federal debt.

This is not simply a matter of fair taxation based on services received. It is a matter of an existential threat to our democratic system. One might think that this is a momentary danger. It is not. As John Adams knew, plutocracy (which he called aristocracy) is always a danger; but Jefferson, Madison, and Hamilton and most of their countrymen denied its existence. As Richard Ryerson points out, Adams could not predict the form of aristocracy in the twenty-first century, but he did foresee the basic form: "grasping wealthy men who would employ any means to political power in order to aggrandize their fortunes" (Ryerson 2016, 430). Here is one example of Adams's concern, from a September 27, 1808, letter to Benjamin Rush:

> I believe, with you, "a republican government," while the people have the virtues, talents, and love of country necessary to support it, "the best possible government to promote the interest, dignity, and happiness of man." But you know that commerce, luxury, and avarice have destroyed every republican government. England and France have tried the experiment, and neither of them could preserve it, for twelve years. . . . When public virtue is gone, when the national spirit is fled, when a party is substituted for the nation and faction for a party, when venality lurks and skulks in secret, and much more when it impudently braves the public censure, whether it be sent in the form of emissaries from foreign powers or is employed by ambitious and intriguing domestic citizens, the republic is lost in essence, though it may still exist in form. (Schutz and Adair 1966, 119–20).

As is obvious from recent events in Washington, his wisdom is not common knowledge. Faction is now more important than what is best for the nation.

Nadia Urbinati made a similar point, quoting Norberto Bobbio's *Future of Democracy*:

> Bobbio warned that the power of economic interests combined with the decline in the political or civic education of citizens might give rise to a mixture lethal to representative democracy: the formation of an oligarchical power that could moreover win legitimization through a public opinion rendered docile, uncritical, and passive or else kept in ignorance and rendered incompetent to judge. (Urbinati 2015, 94).

Individuality within community protects democratic values. But the herd mentality of the protesters in Washington on January 6, 2021, illustrates the danger of mass hysteria. They were mobilized by a narcissist, a man incapable of understanding the value of individuality within community. The protesters that day also illustrate that communities can become lethal. How is one to distinguish between healthy and unhealthy communities? Two metrics might apply in such situations: the love ethic and Gandhian truth. Does the community demonstrate love for the neighbor, and is the community open to the truth that the "other" has?

One aspect of individualism is in plain view—the current Washington stalemate. The founders' restraints on government power, with their revered checks and balances, were a masterful creation to protect against dictatorship; but the system can produce political paralysis when excessive individualism is part of the mix. Add lust for power to politicians' longstanding fear of telling people the truth about taxes and services (you want services, you must pay taxes) and one has a recipe for trouble. Can you imagine what bankruptcy by the United States would do to the world? All because too many politicians do not understand that governments have to pay their bills; to do so, taxes are needed. Tea Party types talk about balancing the budget, but only by cutting services which the American people do not want; furthermore, it is impossible to cut services enough to balance the budget unless one demobilizes much of the military. The difficulty of cutting services is perhaps nowhere more obvious than when Republicans are in power; they cut taxes, but not services.

Given the enormous range and value of community contributions to capitalism, fairness would suggest less individual greed. Sociability, in the form of government, provides many benefits. It is also directly related to increased happiness, which we now examine.

Chapter Six

Sociability and Happiness

Liberty was, obviously, a crucial part of the Founders' justification for independence. But liberty included the revolutionary right for all to pursue happiness. In his influential 1776 essay "Thoughts on Government," John Adams wrote that "the happiness of society is the end of Government. . . . From this principle it will follow, that the form of government, which communicates . . . happiness to the greatest number of persons, and in the greatest degree, is the best" (Taylor, IV 1979, 86). This Enlightenment ideal was radical; all people, not only the wealthy, had a right to seek happiness.

A few years later, Adams again commented on happiness in an October 25, 1781, letter from his diplomatic post in the Netherlands: government should "oblige all to co-operate in this one democratical principle, that the End of all Government is the happiness of the People: and in this other, that the greatest happiness of the greatest Number is the point to be obtained" (Lint 2004, XII 48). Jon Meacham argues that "the pursuit of happiness—the pursuit of the good of the whole, because the good of the whole was crucial to genuine well-being of the individual, and vice versa—became part of the fabric (at first brittle, to be sure, but steadily stronger) of the young nation" (Meacham 2018, 41). Note the yin-yang of community and individual.

The Founders had no models on which to base this experiment in liberty and happiness; there had never been a democracy of such geographic scale and with such inclusive aspirations. Still, the idea of a universal right to pursue happiness was widely accepted among Enlightenment thinkers, as Darrin McMahon clearly states: "To many enlightened souls on both sides of the Atlantic, the need to promote happiness had assumed the status of a self-evident truth" (McMahon 2004, 5). But what country had attempted this? None. The Declaration of Independence was breaking new ground.

However, in the Revolutionary Era, "universal" rights applied only to adult white males. Over time we have moved toward greater inclusion with women's suffrage and expansion of civil rights. But progress has been unconscionably slow on all fronts; two hundred fifty years after the Declaration of Independence, there is far too much discrimination and exclusion. The Founders' revolutionary aspirations have not been fulfilled. We have become a plutocracy.

WEALTH AND HAPPINESS

The reader might, at this point, object that I am ignoring the happiness benefits of great wealth. It is easy to assume that immense wealth buys happiness, but that is not necessarily true. Naomi Oreskes and Eric Conway state that

> Study after study has shown that people are happiest . . . when they live in societies with strong social safety nets and robust family and community ties. Typically that means living in a country with good health provision, with protections to buffer unemployment, and where work is not so all-consuming as to leave inadequate time for family and friends. (Oreskes and Conway 2023, 404).

They note that those whose goal is wealth are less happy than those with other goals.

Happiness scholars argue that enormous annual earnings (setting aside the issue of whether they are merited) do not seem to add much to one's happiness. Money may buy happiness at lower socioeconomic levels, but it has less impact at higher levels. Richard Layard, for instance, notes that "extra income increases happiness less and less as people get richer" (Layard 2005, 231). Bruno Frey writes that "additional income does not increase happiness *ad infinitum*. The relationship between income and happiness is not linear; there is diminishing marginal utility with absolute income" (Frey 2008, 29). Later in the same work, discussing ten essentials of happiness, he argues that "earning more money is very unimportant" (Frey 2008, 151–52). Ed and Robert Diener agree when they state that research on whether money causes happiness "tells us that it is generally good for your happiness to *have* money, but toxic to your happiness to *want* money too much. A high income can help happiness, but is no sure path to it" (Diener and Diener 2008, 111). And Sonja Lyubomirsky points out that wanting more and more money may not have the desired result, stating that materialists are less happy and also more likely "to suffer from a variety of mental disorders!" (Lyubomirsky 2008, 43).

Concentration of wealth, in contrast to Smith's advocacy of diffusing wealth to all classes, may partially explain why happiness in the United States has not increased for decades, even though the economy has grown enormously. Lawrence Samuel, for instance, argues that happiness levels in the United States have been "essentially frozen since the 1950s" (Samuel 2018, 121). That happiness levels have stagnated is supported by the polling of the

National Opinion Research Center (NORC), which shows variation from year to year but very little change over the long term (Smith 2015, 56). Some even argue that Americans have become increasingly depressed in recent decades (Sandler 2011, 70).

This is the Easterlin Paradox:

> Average levels of happiness in the United States have risen very little if at all over the past 50 years despite substantial growth in per capita incomes. Although rich people, as a whole, are happier than poor people and average levels of well-being are almost invariably higher in wealthy nations than in poorer countries, the percentages of Americans who declare themselves "very happy," "pretty happy," or "not too happy" are almost exactly the same as they were half a century ago. (Bok 2010a, 5).

One possible explanation is that Americans work four hours longer per week than people in other advanced economies. This statistic is based on comparing the United States with a group of eleven similar countries, on annual hours worked in 2018. The countries were Canada, Denmark, France, Germany, Israel, Italy, Japan, the Netherlands, Norway, Sweden, and the United Kingdom (my computation, based on OECD, *Statistical Abstracts*). Extra hours at work come at the expense of family and social relationships; this undermines happiness because good social relationships are crucial contributors to happiness.

SOCIABILITY AND HAPPINESS

Close friends and a good marriage are among the social factors connected to happiness noted by Derek Bok. He also writes that "several researchers have concluded that human relationships and connections of all kinds contribute more to happiness than anything else" (Bok 2010a, 17 and 19–20). Another social relationship positively related to happiness is altruism, as Sissela Bok explains: "People who rank high on scales of subjective well-being are also found to be more likely to engage in certain altruistic activities such as volunteering" (Bok 2010b, 53).

The importance of social relationships is not a new idea, according to Haidt:

> Seneca was right: "No one can live happily who has regard to himself alone and transforms everything into a question of his own utility." John Donne was right: No man, woman or child is an island. Aristophanes was right. We need others to complete us. We are an ultrasocial species, full of emotions finely tuned for loving, befriending, helping, sharing, and otherwise intertwining our lives with others. Attachments and relationships can bring us pain: As a

> character in Jean-Paul Sartre's play *No Exit* said, "Hell is other people." But so is heaven. (Haidt 2006, 133–34).

Indeed, Haidt is correct in tracing this idea back thousands of years; here is a more recent source. Adam Smith knew this in the eighteenth century: "Society and conversation, therefore, are the most powerful remedies for restoring the mind to its tranquility, if, at any time, it has unfortunately lost it; as well as the best preservatives of that equal and happy temper, which is so necessary to self-satisfaction and enjoyment" (Smith 1790, I 42–3).

Modern happiness scholars reinforce the importance of sociability. For instance, Ed and Robert Diener write:

> Relationships are themselves a crucial part of psychological wealth without which you cannot be truly rich. Simply put, we need others to flourish. Indeed, the results of research on social relationships and happiness are clear on this point: healthy social contact is essential for happiness. Family relationships and close friendships are important to happiness. Many studies show that happy people are also more blessed with good families, friends, and supportive relationships than are people with low life satisfaction. . . .
>
> Many psychologists think that humans are genetically wired to need one another. (Diener and Diener 2008, 50).

So sociability and happiness are connected. Moreover, good social relations have a positive impact on health. Boccalandro, who analyzes the importance of purposeful work, writes: "The body of existing research unequivocally establishes that social purpose substantially improves our health and wellness, including lowering our risk of suffering from stress, depression, cardiovascular disease and unhappiness" (Boccalandro 2021, 31). Medical researchers have also noted the health-sociability connection: "The data we have presented suggest that health is not as individualistic a concept as people in the United States may assume it to be." Data demonstrate the "individualist vision of health to be incomplete." Among other problems with American health care, they note "overreliance on individualism" and "underinvestment in social capital" (Bradley and Taylor 2013, 194–95).

Many Americans, ignoring what scholars have argued, focus on the self at the expense of sociability. Moreover, increasing individualism has a cost that is not obvious but is quite dangerous, as Urbinati explains:

> The more citizens withdraw from public life in order to occupy themselves with their personal concerns, since individual rights serve their purpose here, the more the feeling of solidarity with others declines, the more that quality of empathy which, as we have seen, is among the components of democratic

> individualism, dries up, the more the political order is exposed to the risks of despotism and a curtailment of liberty, not through an excess of politics, but through an atrophying of politics. (Urbinati 2015, 120).

Note Urbinati's statement of the danger of democratic atrophy; I have argued that democracy has been transmuted into plutocratic despotism in the United States. And it is not hard to find real examples of this decline in other countries (Hungary and the Philippines come readily to mind).

Withdrawal from the public sphere has a negative impact on happiness. Contemporary happiness scholars argue that participation in politics increases happiness in two ways. Bruno Frey writes that democracy provides "the people with more desirable political decisions (outcome utility)." In addition, participating in politics provides a happiness benefit that Frey labels procedural utility (Frey 2008, 61). Participating in decisions affecting your own life increases happiness, and the results of the democratic process also add happiness.

This was shown in the 1970s in the Judith Rodin and Ellen Langer experiment with nursing home residents. In a more recent book, Langer discusses the experiment, in which two groups of residents were given plants. Staff took care of the plants for the control group. In the other group, residents were given some autonomy plus "responsibility over a plant that resulted in significant differences on measures of alertness, happiness, active participation, and a general sense of well-being just three weeks later. Eighteen months later, these differences had grown to not just measures of physical and psychological health but also mortality rates" (Langer 2009, 163). Self-rule (even something as simple as control of a house plant) has health as well as happiness benefits.

That citizens have been withdrawing from the public sphere needs emphasis. Community organizations have struggled in recent decades as Putnam makes crystal clear in several books. In *Our Kids,* he notes a study by scholars skeptical of his *Bowling Alone* findings; the skeptics intended to refute his study but instead confirmed his findings; they reported "that both kin and nonkin networks have shrunk in the past two decades, but that the decrease in nonkin networks was greater" (Putnam 2015, 211).

That community functions in the United States are impoverished is something I have often felt while traveling in Europe. What always impresses me about European nations is the ubiquity of superb examples of community. Over the centuries and still today, large numbers of people working for the common good have produced many useful and beautiful things—from Roman aqueducts to modern mass transit systems. And one must not omit the magnificent architecture throughout Europe. One is amazed by the splendor of the Pitti Palace, the Medici Chapel and San Lorenzo Basilica in Florence, numerous other cathedrals, and the gorgeous churches even in smaller towns throughout Europe. So much of this was accomplished in grossly unequal, unfree societies. Think of what could be accomplished by democratic individuals within democratic communities.

So people working together on massive projects can, given enough time, do marvelous things. This is hardly news. And it is also not news that so much of this was accomplished by thoroughly repressive regimes—both secular and religious. All that glorious beauty both before and after the barbarian invasions of Europe has repeatedly left me disquieted. The repression needed to accomplish these things—whether by church or state—is, to say the least, unsettling. But there are also examples of democratic societies working together and accomplishing great things. The community spirit of World War II in the United States, transitioning from the miniscule military of a geographically isolated country to world leadership that, in four years, along with allies, defeated two militarily powerful nations, is one example. Europe rebuilding after World War II and transforming into the European Union is another.

Obviously, modern, egalitarian democracies are not compatible with the social control of earlier ages. But have we gone too far in the opposite direction? Have we lost the value of community in our quest for individual autonomy? Are we less happy as a result? How can one balance the benefits of community and the benefits of individuality? How can we move beyond the myth of individualism (a myth because no rugged individualist is self-sufficient) to individuality within symbiotic communities? Can one even be a complete person outside of community?

CONCLUSION

Individualistic capitalism is not the only available option for democratic market societies. Smith's emphasis on justice and sociability suggests that we have underemphasized community. This may seem irrational to believers in Friedman's shareholder-value capitalism, but replacing such selfish individualism with altruism might serve our country well. According to Robert Frank,

> Altruists . . . appear to do better economically: the experimental studies consistently find that altruistic behavior is positively correlated with socioeconomic status. Of course, this does not mean that altruistic behavior necessarily *causes* economic success. But it does suggest that an altruistic posture cannot be too seriously burdensome in material terms (Frank 1988, 235).

Individualism is a social pathology that is harming American society in numerous ways. It actively impedes racial reconciliation, and it exacerbates class differences. Smith understood that increased productivity resulting from the division of labor makes it possible to diffuse wealth to the lowest classes. Failure to act on that subtle hint means that economic inequity worsens; billionaires get richer while people struggle with homelessness.

The three misinterpretations also affect American happiness. Nordic countries, for instance, regularly are ranked as happier than the United States. Given the connection between sociability and increased happiness, there is reason to suggest that this country could have both a sounder economy and more widely diffused happiness if it were less individualistic. It might also be healthier. Demonstrating that connection, however, is not within the scope of this work.

How could we be more sociable? The next chapter will examine some examples of individuality within community. Ethical capitalism is not a utopian fantasy.

Conclusion

Belying our democratic pretensions, individualism has produced plutocracy, which has broken an intergenerational compact, bequeathing an enormous debt to our descendants by reducing taxes without also reducing government expenditures. This injustice of passing on our debts would end if the wealthy paid fair taxes instead of, often, less than the middle class and if the resulting tax revenues were directed to an increase in services for the middle and working classes and to a robust plan to repay the federal debt. Merely repaying the debt is insufficient for providing equal opportunity. Health care, education, and social services have been underfunded for years; an enhanced local, state, and federal role is needed to remedy these deficits in order to provide a level playing field. But we will never be able to repay the debt and provide needed government services if taxes are seen as a form of theft. As Chapter 5 illustrates, the government provides myriad services; in effect, we the people are providing these services to ourselves. A more sociable America would have taxes sufficient to pay current expenses, plus enough to retire the debt in a reasonable period of time. Deficit spending would be an emergency tool, not standard practice.

Sociability, the individuality within communities advocated in this book, is not new; the Pilgrims were individuals who survived because of community. But Americans have become more individualistic since the initial settlers. We have ignored the sociable political-economy Smith advocated; we do not follow the "Love your neighbor as yourself" commandment; we are not aware of John Adams's warnings about aristocracy. Our political economy has become a plutocracy in which a few billionaires wage class warfare against the middle and working classes. Our society is individualistic at the expense of community. At the same time, much remains to be done on race and gender issues.

Team sports demonstrate that a different approach is possible. Teams fail at the highest level if players are interested only in personal statistics, but they win championships when they cohere as a unit. Players do not have to surrender their individuality; fans and players pay close attention to personal statistics, stars are rewarded with multimillion-dollar, multiyear contracts, personal traits are grist for sports writers, and individual accomplishments are celebrated. But those feats are more valued when they contribute to victories and championships at the end of the season. Winning a championship is accomplished not by individualism, but by a cohesive combination of individuals, making team sports a good example of the yin-yang of individuality within community.

For example, the 2018 Boston Red Sox won the World Series because they transcended individualism to become a team. Many reasons can be given for that spectacular success. Leaders were respectful of the diverse individuals on the team; players reciprocated that respect. Modern analytics were blended with emotion and feel for the game. Perhaps most important, many strong people submerged their individualism to support the team's quest for the World Series. It did not matter that players were of various ethnicities and came from several countries in addition to the United States: Aruba, the Dominican Republic, Mexico, and Venezuela. What mattered was that everyone bought into the team concept.

This will not surprise anyone who has ever played a team sport; coaches emphasize group cohesion over individual accomplishment. That approach is sometimes forgotten, but successful teams implement it. Individual competitiveness of each player is not diminished by the emphasis on community, but the "I" of individualism is abandoned for the greater good.

But how does the Red Sox winning a World Series connect with Adam Smith, religion, and John Adams? A flourishing economy requires individuals striving for success; when that striving is within the bounds of Smith's sociability, justice, and equality, it is consistent with community, with liberty for everyone, not just a favored few. Our recession-prone economy would be stronger if it were a sociable market, not the individualistic market that we currently have. Christianity requires individual salvation, but it brings the individual into a new community and commands adherents to love one's neighbor. Community played a large role in the establishment and development of this nation. Adams was an individual, but he was firmly embedded in multiple communities. He sacrificed personal comfort and suffered long separations from his beloved family as a community servant.

The importance of teamwork is clear to some economists; for instance, Joseph Stiglitz, the 2001 Nobel Prize winner in economics, wrote:

> The reason that economic theory failed to gauge accurately the effectiveness of team incentives is that it underestimated the importance of personal connectedness. Individuals work hard to please others in their team—and because they believe it is the right thing to do. Economists overestimate, too, the selfishness of individuals (though there is considerable evidence that economists are more selfish than others, and that economics training does make individuals more selfish over time). It is thus perhaps not surprising that firms owned by their

> workers—and who therefore share in the profits—have performed better in the crisis and laid off fewer employees. (Stiglitz 2012, 113).

Ernst Fehr and Simon Gachter argue that the pure self-interest model, while useful, is inadequate; "a sizeable proportion of economic actors act on considerations of reciprocity" (Fehr and Gachter 2000, 22). And remember Jonathan Haidt's emphasis on reciprocity, noted in Chapter 1.

The sports analogy should not be carried too far. Only one team wins in sports—but in economics and politics those who play zero-sum games reduce the possibilities for everyone else. In other words, individualists playing zero-sum games accumulate disproportionate benefits, but community-oriented societies spread the wealth. Billionaires add to their billions so they can make touristic space trips, meanwhile decreasing the marginal propensity to consume, weakening the economy, and undermining the quality of life for the rest of the population. Those teams called political parties often forget that their purpose is to serve the entire community, not only their particular faction. Parties often disparage their opponent's love of country, campaign for office 24/7/365 at the expense of governing for the common good, and translate elections, the means of gaining power in a democracy, into their reason for existence. A win-win approach would be better for the economy and for our democracy.

The cynic may sneer at community in competitive sports, wondering what that has to do with the real business of life, economics. But there are other examples.

COOPERATIVES IN THE UNITED STATES

Sociable economies work in Scandinavian and other European nations, several of which include workers' representatives on corporate boards. Thomas Piketty argues,

> Nothing guarantees that stockholders are more competent to manage an enterprise than a company's employees, or that they are more invested in its success over the long term. Often, the opposite is true: an investment fund can put capital into an enterprise and withdraw it again in a short period of time, whereas employees generally invest a major part of their lives, their energy, and their skills. (Piketty 2022, 113).

There is no reason that workers should not own businesses. But the critic counters that what works well in small, relatively homogenous nations is not applicable to the much larger and more heterogeneous United States.

The critic would be wrong; cooperative economic relations were part of the founding of this nation. Benjamin Franklin's mutual fire insurance cooperative began business in 1752 and is still functioning today. That he did not patent any of his inventions because he wanted them to be available for everyone further demonstrates his community consciousness. Tocqueville commented on individuals working together, both for personal benefit and for the good of the community, in nineteenth century America (Putnam 2020, 1–2). For example, cooperative marketing and purchasing benefited many farmers in the 1800s.

Perhaps the critic is unaware of the importance of cooperatives in this nation. A decade ago, Gar Alperowitz wrote about the number of cooperative economic organizations in the United States, with 40 percent of Americans as members of agricultural co-ops, insurance co-ops, retail co-ops, and credit unions (Alperovitz, 2013, 35). The National Cooperative Business Association/CLUSA International lists a wide variety of member organizations, such as credit unions, grocery stores, housing, rural telecommunications, electricity co-ops, farmers' unions, and supply co-ops (National Cooperative Business Association/CLUSA 2021). Welders, for instance, can join the Independent Welding and Gas Distributors (IWDC), a purchasing and marketing cooperative with eight hundred members throughout North America (Independent Welding Distributors Cooperative 2021). Sara Horowitz lists four types of "mutualist" organizations: "Religious organizations, mutual aid societies, cooperatives, and labor organizations" (Horowitz 2021, 64–5 and 181). Habitat for Humanity should also be noted. And even the world of sports provides an example of a cooperatively owned professional athletic franchise—the Green Bay Packers (Horowitz 2021, 198–99).

In addition to the significant number of cooperatives in the United States, there are many flourishing contemporary examples in other countries, such as Mondragon in Spain and Emilia-Romagna in Italy. These large, complex, cooperative economic systems compete effectively both within their national markets and in international trade (Solimano 2014, 162–64). Worldwide, diverse cooperatives do a significant amount of business. If co-ops were a country they would be the seventh-largest economy in the world (Lakey 2017, 95). "According to the International Cooperative Alliance (ICA), in cooperation with the United Nations, around 1 billion people worldwide are members of a cooperative" (Solimano 2014, 163–64). And they are relatively successful in the market economy; according to George Lakey, they are less likely to go bankrupt, having "only one-third the chance of failing compared with public companies" (Lakey 2017, 96).

Cooperative living arrangements demonstrate individuality within community: cohousing, purely as a housing option or as part of a religious community provides an American example. Several such sociable religious communities have existed in this country, some continuously for decades. Some have individual family living arrangements within robust community structures (Jackson 2009). In recent years, cohousing has been marketed to senior citizens in several western states.

Sojourners in Washington, DC, in existence for more than fifty years, exemplifies community. Two of its leaders characterize it as follows: "The beloved community is one in which people of different backgrounds recognize that our individual well-being is inextricably linked to the well-being of others. It is a society built upon and committed to extending liberty and justice for all and that embraces interdependence, empathy, and love" (Wallis and Taylor 2020).

In short, diverse community organizations have existed in the United States for centuries. A more community-oriented market economy would not be un-American or a reinvention of the wheel.

What I am suggesting would not require revolutionary changes. Cooperative membership need not be universal; for it to be compatible with individuality, it would be voluntary. It would be compatible with Smith's sociable and just market economy and consistent with both our religious roots and the ideals that the founders of this nation fought to establish.

A PLEA FOR THE COMMON GOOD

When individuals are part of communities, everyone benefits. The yin-yang of individuality within communities is better for all than the excessive individualism that prevails in the United States today. Throughout this work I have argued that the ideals of our founders, the ideals spelled out in the Declaration of Independence and the Preamble to the Constitution, require a more community-oriented society. This would provide some inoculation against dictatorship and be beneficial for happiness. Democracy is difficult to maintain, as has been demonstrated in several countries that have regressed into autocracy in recent decades. Wealth is also undermining our democracy, twisting it into an aristocracy.

Politics has become a winner-take-all game. But then what happens to the losing party? History is replete with civil disturbances and wars resulting from decades of such politics piling up grievances against the winners. In the eighteenth century, the United States was a relatively exclusive political culture; only white males were included. Immigration brought cultural diversity, but equal rights for all in this diverse nation is an incomplete project. New groups have struggled for decades, and some are still striving for equal rights. As the United States has diversified, the impetus to exclude others has gotten stronger. Those others might be of a different political party, ethnicity, religion, sexual orientation, socio-economic class, or other factors. The exclusivity of such groups is incompatible with the inclusivity of the love ethic.

Does an election victory give any party the right to promote its agenda at the expense of the common good? This can be problematic if a group with a winner-take-all attitude controls one of the many veto points in our system (House, Senate, Supreme Court, and presidency). Such partisanship can prevent government action. Extreme partisanship, evident in the events of January 6, 2021, could threaten constitutional government in the United States. Intolerance of political opponents, including violent confrontation, demonstrates that the trust a vibrant democracy requires has been seriously eroded. We might take the advice of a Conservative Party member of Britain's Parliament "to recreate a political middle ground, a shared sense of the common good" (Norman 2018, 301). Perhaps I am naïve to think that the United States could do that, but I still have faith that democracy can be restored. The Progressive Era, the New Deal, and the Civil Rights Movement provide examples.

More than 150 years after the Civil War, we have not rectified the inequities of America's original sin. Individualism has impeded racial reconciliation, as Putnam explains: "One lesson of the complex history of race in twentieth-century America is perhaps simply this: 'We' can be defined in more inclusive or exclusive terms, and that inclusiveness can gradually change over time. But a selfish, fragmented 'I' society is not a favorable environment for achieving racial equality" (Putnam 2020, 244). We need to move from an individualistic society to a more sociable "individuality in communities" society.

Our political elitism has consistently privileged the already privileged, at the expense of long-standing needs of the middle and working classes, such as college tuition debt, equitable healthcare, and long-term unemployment and under-employment. Consider the three tax bonanzas for the wealthy enacted in the Reagan, George W. Bush, and Trump administrations; all were labeled trickle-down policies that would benefit all Americans. But the benefits somehow did not trickle down; instead, they were gushers rising to the top, exacerbating the national debt, and starving the government of funds needed to address community needs. Blatant denial of climate change is, similarly, a dangerous rejection of governing for all the people.

Excessive individualism is also manifest in international relations, varying with the occupant of the Oval Office. The myth that hard-headed (realist) foreign policy leaders should be concerned with the national interest first and foremost, that the United States alone can determine and protect its national interest, blinds us to the potential for cooperation with other nations. And so the United States has been loath to invest in developing the cooperative international community potential of the United Nations. In short, we have, too often, tried to solve international problems alone, imposing our solutions on the rest of the world. Vietnam and Iraq are two notable examples. Time will tell if collaboration with NATO in assisting Ukraine indicates a more community-oriented foreign policy.

SOME CHARACTERISTICS OF INDIVIDUALITY WITHIN COMMUNITIES

What would sociable communities look like? People would be aware of multiple connections with a variety of groups but comfortable in themselves, striving for personal excellence while supporting others as they strive for their own goals. They would be just societies in which all individuals could flourish. But for all individuals to be able to flourish, they must work together. John Campbell and John Hall suggest "rejuvenating social democratic parties and trade unions but also engaging churches, nonprofit organizations, nongovernmental agencies, volunteer organizations and civic groups. Only organization can create an effective countermovement to corporate power" (Campbell and Hall 2021, 206). Edith Rasell reminds us that government also has an important role: "Government done right can protect and advance the common good, including broadly shared prosperity. . . . A just economy is possible only if the public, using the tool that is government, makes it happen" (Rasell 2022, 165).

What would it mean to have a just society? It would not have a free market economy, but it would have a market economy consistent with Smith's thinking, a sociable, ethical and equal opportunity market. Piketty offers a definition (which he admits is imperfect):

> A just society is one that allows all its members access to the widest possible range of fundamental goods. Fundamental goods include education, health, the right to vote, and more generally to participate as fully as possible in the various forms of social, cultural, economic, civic, and political life. A just society organizes socioeconomic relations, property rights, and the distribution of income and wealth in such a way as to allow its least advantaged members to enjoy the highest possible life conditions. (Piketty 2020, 967–68).

Note that allowing everybody "access to the widest possible range of fundamental goods" would require significant change in our economic thinking. While protecting individuality, societal sources of advantage for the wealthy (such as a tax code that allows billionaires to pay a lower tax rate than the middle class) and disadvantage for the working classes (such as crushing tuition debts) would be eliminated. A fair system would be consistent with religious values and with Smith's sociable market. As Rasell notes, "We largely view meeting human needs as an individual responsibility even though Jesus and the biblical writers teach that society is obligated to ensure the well-being of all" (Rasell 2022, 209). She also argues, "Economic security comes through community and only through community" (Rasell 2022, 210).

The greed of corporate CEOs would be tamed. Corporate boards are supposed to determine CEO compensation, but that assumes board members are independent of the CEO. Many board members are political captives of the CEO. Thus, they are unable to base CEO pay on real contributions to the corporation. Legislation limiting the ratio of CEO compensation to average worker pay might be one solution. If change either by corporate boards or by legislation does not occur, we would have clear evidence that this country has become what Adams feared, an aristocracy, not a democracy.

In Piketty's just society, income would be distributed more fairly. The working and middle classes would be well off, consistent with Smith's insight that increased productivity, due to the division of labor, makes it possible to diffuse wealth to the lowest ranks of the people. Assuming a more progressive tax structure and more reasonable compensation for CEOs, closer to the 20:1 ratio that J. P. Morgan thought was the upper limit, excessive wealth would probably disappear but there would still be wealthy people. The improved economic status of working and middle class people would contribute to better health and happiness metrics. The diminished economic standing of the wealthy would not affect their health; they would still have the resources for a robust pursuit of the good life. Individualistic greed would be tamed but probably not shrink away to nothingness.

A different view of the role of profit would also be needed. It should be seen as a metric of success, not the goal. Businesses exist to provide a product or a service; profit is a measure of how well that is done. In recent decades this product orientation has been forgotten, with shareholder value putting profit above all else; the metric has become the goal. Individualistic CEOs have been heedless of community impact while laying waste to viable enterprises. Profit is certainly important as a measure of success, but as the goal, it has been destructive. This is perhaps most obvious in that casino known as Wall Street. The ideology of a free market economy would be replaced by a just market economy, consistent with Smith's sociability, with the Christian love ethic, and a reasonable response to Adams's warnings of the danger of aristocracy.

It should be obvious from earlier chapters that the greed of individualistic plutocrats is not acceptable in a society of individuality within communities. This is not a blanket condemnation of wealthy people, but a plea for them to be good citizens, which includes paying fair taxes, not grasping for special privileges or despoiling the environment in the quest for more wealth.

After all, Adam Smith saw the wealthy as a valuable part of society, providing a model for people to aspire to. There would still be wealthy people, but as Smith suggested they would pay higher taxes and wealth would be widely diffused.

In addition to economic changes, there are policy changes that would contribute to greater sociability. This book would be significantly longer if all such changes were catalogued, but here are two examples. Care for the environment to improve living conditions today and to maintain a habitable earth for future generations is imperative. Investing more in education would increase social cohesion. According to Heather Boushey, improving education would significantly benefit families and the economy. She states that "studies are so rigorous and, by now, so numerous that the conclusion is beyond reasonable debate. Fortunately, they are generating a broad consensus that investments in education—especially early childhood education—are in the national interest" (Boushey 2019, 54–5). The cost of higher education would also be addressed. Between our founding and the early twentieth century, publicly funded education was gradually expanded from primary school up to the twelfth grade; this was one reason for our strong economic growth as a nation. But extension to higher grades stopped at the senior year of high school. How many potential Einsteins have been unable to reach their potential because of the cost of a university education?

The United States is wealthy enough to end poverty. Matthew Desmond argues that we could do that without increasing the deficit if the IRS enforced the tax code and "cracked down on corporations and families who cheat on their taxes, reallocating the newfound revenue to those most in need of it. . . . We could afford it if the well-off among us took less from the government. We could afford it if we designed our welfare state to expand opportunity and not guard fortunes" (Desmond 2023, 147–49).

Individualistic certitude that one has a monopoly on the truth would be replaced by openness to truths held by people with diverse opinions. Second Amendment rights provide an example of how this might work. A more community-oriented gun owner would accept an argument that balances a right to some (but not all) arms while allowing society more security. The amendment states: "A well-regulated militia being necessary to the security of a free state, the right of the people to keep and bear arms shall not be infringed." Ignoring the premise of the amendment and emphasizing its conclusion, gun enthusiasts and Supreme Court justices have interpreted it individualistically. The result has been thousands of deaths and injuries from gun violence every year. However, the Second Amendment can be interpreted so that gun rights are compatible with community safety, significantly reducing the obscene number of deaths and injuries by firearms.

The Founders saw a standing army as a threat to freedom; they knew that militia had played a significant role in winning independence from Britain. So constitutional enshrinement of the need for a militia made sense in the eighteenth century. The people's right to weapons was important for rapid mobilization of a volunteer force to defend the nation. Militia were important at that time, and we continued to rely on them for protection for almost two centuries. However, when United States territory was directly attacked in 1941, a standing army, not a militia, was needed. Since the 1940s, that standing army (or diplomacy as in President Kennedy's prevention of a nuclear holocaust in the Cuban Missile Crisis) has provided our defense. Every year, anachronistic interpretation of an amendment meant to protect freedom deprives thousands of Americans of their most basic freedom, the right to life.

This argument will elicit a reflex response that I am ignoring the Second Amendment. That is not the case; I am well aware of the words used to enable lethal gun violence but consider them to be subordinate to the purpose spelled out in the amendment: "the security of a free State." What is plain to see is that unregulated, heavily armed individuals are wreaking havoc in our society, undermining the security of free citizens, while adding nothing to national security. Supporters of virtually unlimited Second Amendment rights illustrate the individualism virus infecting our body politic; their insensitivity to victims of gun violence shows disregard for community. Can we really argue that our nation is safe under the current individualistic interpretation? There must be a better balance of the individual right to bear arms and community rights, consistent with the Constitution. But that would require the Supreme Court to base its judgment on the entire amendment.

An individuality within communities argument recognizes that sportsmen and hunters have rights, but the people as a whole also have rights. The people certainly have a right to defense against foreign invasion which the government provided in World War II. A nation divided on the issue of war came together as a national community; the government, not a militia, supplied the weapons for a rapidly expanded regular army. Equally certain is that people have rights to security from the lethal violence of military equipment in the hands of unregulated individuals. "A well-regulated militia" is still part of the Second Amendment.

This is only one of many important issues that demonstrate our societal emphasis on individualism. There is no need to catalog the issues; the reader probably already has a list in mind. A commonality of these issues is a conviction that one has the absolute truth and the opponent is completely wrong. But such a perspective runs the danger of missing part of the truth. Piketty writes that "No one will ever possess the absolute truth about just ownership, just borders, just democracy, just taxes and education" (Piketty 2020, 1036). We all need to be open to the truth held by the other side.

STRATEGY

How do we change to a more just society? Violent revolution, an individualistic approach, would not be advisable. It acts on the mantra of revolutionaries, such as Frantz Fanon, Lenin, Mao Zedong, Che Guevara, that the only way for a MAN to respond to injustice is to join with people of like mind, take up arms and fight. This might sound like individuals working within communities to rectify injustice, but the problem is that it assumes that the revolutionaries are right and the opposition is wrong, inhumane, perhaps evil. While the injustice is often very real, violent change denies the humanity of the opponent. And the victors often inflict new harm.

Without taking a stand in absolute opposition to revolutionary change, we should take to heart the position of Smith (and his close friend, Hume):

> They both distrusted large and sudden innovations in politics. Given the fallibility of human reason and the complicated variable nature of the political world, they held, we should be wary of grand schemes for radically restructuring society. Hence, while they advocated certain reforms to the society of their day—freer trade and greater religious toleration, for instance—they always insisted that these changes should be implemented in a gradual, measured way. (Rasmussen 2017, 13).

Consistent with Smith and Hume and with our values, this work favors significant but evolutionary societal change that eliminates the individualistic greed that is destroying our society and our economy; this would result in greater social mobility and more concern for the common good.

Such gradual change may not always be the best approach; for instance, it was necessary to take up arms in the American War for Independence and in response to fascism in World War II. But, too often violence causes more harm than good. There is another way to fight, a way that can be, and very often has been, very effective—nonviolent resistance. Gandhi is only one of many successful practitioners of this potent political strategy as Peter Ackerman and Jack Duvall (in *A Force More Powerful*) and Erica Chenoweth and Maria Stephan (in *Why Civil Resistance Works*) document with multiple examples. Chenoweth and Stephan's statistical analysis of nonviolent actions, in contrast with violent movements, demonstrates the superiority of nonviolence for resolving problems.

Some may object that nonviolence, while a good strategy, would not work in Muslim societies because so many recent terrorists have come from that culture. But that may be a hasty judgment. Only a very small percentage of Muslims have been terrorists; the overwhelming majority of Muslims are peaceful. Gandhi had Muslim allies and aides (Abdul Ghaffar Khan and

Maulana Azad, for instance) and more recently Ibrahim Rugovo of Albania demonstrated its applicability for Muslims. An analogous argument would be that nonviolence would never work for Christians, given how much murder and mayhem has been committed by Christians against other Christians in the wars of the Protestant Reformation, to say nothing of centuries of anti-Semitic violence and the Christian pretensions of the KKK. One must note that such violence contravenes the spirit of Christianity (a point that Muslim scholars would also make about Islam).

Injustice must be fought, but doing so does not require armed struggle. A nonviolent response, as used by Gandhi, King, and myriad others has been highly successful and is respectful of their adversary's humanity. Gandhian nonviolence is significant not only because it is sensitive to the rights of the opposition and of innocent bystanders—but also because it recognizes that the opponent might have part of the truth. As one struggles to find truth, one does not want to destroy those who have ever so small a piece of it. In short, nonviolence delegitimizes the harming of opponents and innocents; it is the love ethic in operation. Applying the love ethic minimizes the action-reaction cycle that violence often ensures.

Nonviolence does not require one to accept injustice passively. There is nothing passive about this form of resistance, which must be both active and persistent to succeed. However, even though its power has been amply demonstrated by Gandhi, King, and others, it is still rejected too readily.

Most people are not activists like King, but we can all work together to strengthen democracy. A more sociable society would be more equitable and democratic. It would respond to John Adams's concern about the aristocrats by preventing any class from dominating; that means the system would have to be "one-person, one vote," not "one dollar, one vote." Transitioning to that more equal democracy will be a long process, but it begins with correcting our mistaken interpretations of capitalism and Christianity, and alertness of the danger of aristocracy.

And a more democratic government would tame casino capitalism, making the market economy efficient for Main Street. That would not eliminate Wall Street, but would restore it to its capital-raising purpose, with profits as the metric of success, not the goal.

SOME FINAL THOUGHTS

Gandhi believed the opponent might have part of the truth. But awareness of the many-sidedness of truth did not prevent Gandhi from struggling tenaciously for his goals; his recognition of the other as holding some of the truth gave his campaigns a different tone. Sociability, humility, and tenacity were a powerful recipe that gained India independence from Britain, without making an enemy of the imperial power.

We should not assume that more sociability would be detrimental to liberty; but too much individualism can produce a war of all against all. Liberty without checks would result in most of us becoming slaves to the few. In contrast, individuality within communities has its benefits. For just one example: happiness scholars have repeatedly demonstrated the positive impact of social relationships on happiness and well-being.

We must maintain individuality but not at the expense of community; implementing Smith's formula of justice, liberty, and equality, would enable this. But who will do this? Almost a century ago, James T. Adams reminded us that it will not be done for us: "Just so long as wealth and power are our sole badges of success, so long will ambitious men strive to attain them" (Adams 1932, 415). We the people must restore a democratic community. The wealthy and powerful will not do it for us.

Having read this far, you may wonder what can one individual do? Many years ago, at a party, I made the host very uneasy by discussing the injustice of free market capitalism. After I argued too long, the host cried out, almost plaintively, "But what do you expect me to do?" I had no answer for him then, but now I think I have an answer that is easy to state but harder to implement: live as an individual within communities, be a loving, community-minded, empathetic person, be a good neighbor. Everyone has a role.

More than that, each of us has a moral responsibility to advocate for equal rights, especially the right to personal fulfillment, however one defines that and assuming no conflict with the right of others to pursue their personal fulfillment.

Appreciate how much we each benefit from the many forms of community. If you are religious, celebrate the variety of religions the Almighty has provided humanity. Be true to your religion while accepting the rich tapestry of faiths, the multiple options that are evidence of God's beneficence. Remember the love ethic; but more important, apply it to those with whom you disagree. Christians believe that Christianity is the only true religion; Muslims believe that Islam has the ultimate truth. Adherents to all religions believe their religion alone is true. But has there ever been and can there ever be a human being who can comprehend what the Almighty intends?

Implicitly, this work has a national focus, but the entire world is one big community of communities. Carl Sandburg noted, talking about global humanity, that "Lincoln used the phrase, 'The Family of Man.' He saw that family as a unity. He hoped to see it move toward closer unity and wider freedom—everywhere" (Sandburg preface, in Basler 1946, xx–xxi). For the future generations of our nation and of the world, our individuality, our freedom, must be embedded in this wider community.

The synthesis of opposites, the yin-yang of individuality within communities, might sound as if everything is relative, but that would be a crude distortion of the argument. Adam Smith suggested an ideal: "to restrain our selfish, and to indulge our benevolent affections, constitutes the perfection of human nature" (Smith 1790, I 47). We are individuals, but Smith's sociability makes us individuals within communities, aiming for perfection, acting in accord with what the impartial spectator approves; such people are sociable, not individualistic.

We would be wise to take Smith's advice to learn from other countries. While discussing Britain's rivalry with France, he stated that other nations' improvements in agriculture, manufacturing, infrastructure "are all proper objects of national emulation, not of national prejudice or envy" (Smith 1790, II 98). That France's agriculture was not particularly advanced in Smith's time may indicate that he was making this point sardonically, rather than advocating a specific French agricultural policy. But the point is worth emphasizing: adapt good ideas, even from your enemies. Instead of being self-centered, so certain that whatever the United States does is best, we should be open to best practices, wherever they originate. There is more problem-solving mental power in the world as a whole than there is in one nation, no matter how creative we are.

Add to Smith's sociability a good dose of Christian love and one would have a different world. As fallible humans, we must apply the love ethic, so clearly specified by Christian scriptures, to the best of our abilities. The love ethic is incompatible with the racism that has so harmed our nation, with the greedy acquisitiveness of the wealthy, with our slow response to global warming. All these are examples of individualistic excess undermining the American dream.

In a letter from the Netherlands dated October 2, 1780, a few years before factions congealed into parties and defeated his presidential reelection bid, Adams wrote, "There is nothing I dread So much, as a Division of the Republick into two great Parties, each arranged under its Leader, and concerting Measures in opposition to each other. This, in my humble Apprehension is to be dreaded as the greatest political Evil, under our Constitution" (Lint 1996, X, 192). Factions see the other as wrong, possibly evil, but we are all members of the diverse American community which is only one part of the human race.

Much as Adams preferred a political system without factions, parties are a fact of life. But they could exist within community. How would that work? They would continue to fight election battles with all their resources. They would not make baseless claims of stolen elections, but would work together to ensure that election results were valid. And, after Election Day, the agenda would shift from electioneering to governing. That governing truce, a patriotic contribution to benefit the entire community, is called bipartisanship.

This country needs a politics of the greater good, in contrast to the contemporary politics of special interests. We need politicians who think of the country instead of fattening their campaign bank accounts. And, for part of each legislative session, we need Congress to focus on working together for the common good. This requires a change of mindset from "my re-election, 24/7/365" to "cooperating with others, legislating to solve problems."

Democracy is about governing for all the people, not solely about getting elected. But campaigning is so expensive that many elected officials are dependent on their donors, unable to vote their conscience. Elections are obviously important, but in a democracy, they are the means, not the end. Is the goal, good governance, also a good election strategy?

How often do politicians vote for the best policy if they fear that it will cost them re-election? Voting for what is best for the community might be contrary to individual interest. But are the two incompatible? Robert Putnam, a scholar of public policy, argues that community/individual dualism is not a "zero-sum trade-off between communitarian equality and individualistic freedom. While we acknowledge this timeless tension, we do not believe that we must choose one side or the other, or that all virtue lies at one pole" (Putnam 2020, 339–40).

There is no easy reset, but as more and more people combine Smith's sociability, justice, equal opportunity, and liberty with Christian love and Adams's skepticism about faction and "aristocrats," the result will be a society in which each person can develop as an individual within strong overlapping communities—an equal democracy with a robust market allowing people of all races, classes, and genders to thrive because no race, class, or gender dominates. This would be a good society.

Bibliography

Ackerman, Peter, and Jack Duvall. 2000. *A Force More Powerful: A Century of Nonviolent Conflict.* New York: Palgrave.

Adams, James Truslow. 1932. *The Epic of America.* Boston: Little, Brown, and Company.

Adams, John Quincy, and Charles Francis Adams. 1980 (1871). *John Adams*, 2 vols. New York: Chelsea House.

Alperovitz, Gar. 2013. *What Then Must We Do: Straight talk about the next American Revolution.* White River Junction, Vermont: Chelsea Green Publishing.

Anderson, Sarah, and Sam Pizzigati. 2022. *Executive excess 2022, Twenty-Eighth annual IPS Executive Compensation Report.* Washington, DC: Institute for Policy Studies.

Arrighi, Giovanni. 2007. *Adam Smith in Beijing: Lineages of the Twenty-First Century.* New York: Verso.

Barker-Benfield, G. J. 2010. *Abigail and John Adams: The Americanization of Sensibility.* Chicago: University of Chicago Press.

Barrera, Albino. 2013. *Biblical Economic Ethics: Sacred Scripture's Teachings on Economic Life.* Lanham, MD: Lexington Books.

Basler, Roy P., ed. 1946. *Abraham Lincoln, His Speeches and Writings.* Cleveland, OH: Da Capo Press.

Beckfield, Jason, and Clare Bambra. 2016. "Shorter lives in stingier states: Social policy shortcomings help explain the US mortality disadvantage." *Social Science & Medicine* 171 (December): 30–8.

Bellah, Robert N., Richard Madsen, William M. Sullivan, Ann Swidler, and Steven M. Lipton. 1985. *Habits of the Heart: Individualism and Commitment in American Life.* New York: Harper and Row.

Bernasek, Anna. 2010. *The Economics of Integrity: From Dairy Farmers to Toyota, How Wealth Is Built on Trust and What That Means for Our Future.* New York: HarperStudio.

Bivens, Josh. 2017. "Inequality is slowing U.S. economic growth: Faster wage growth for low- and middle-wage workers is the solution." Economic Policy Institute (December 12).

Boccalandro, Bea. 2021. *Do Good at Work: How Simple Acts of Social Purpose Drive Success and Wellbeing.* New York: Morgan James Publishing.

Bok, Derek. 2010a. *The Politics of Happiness: What Government Can Learn from the New Research on Well-being.* Princeton, NJ: Princeton University Press.

Bok, Sissela. 2010b. *Exploring Happiness: From Aristotle to Brain Science.* New Haven, CT: Yale University Press.

Bondurant, Joan V. 1971. *Conquest of Violence: The Gandhian Philosophy of Conflict*, rev. ed. Berkeley: University of California Press.

Boorstin, Daniel J. 1966. *An American Primer.* New York: Penguin Books.

Boushey, Heather. 2019. *Unbound, How Inequality Constricts our Economy and What We Can Do about it.* Cambridge, MA: Harvard University Press.

Bradley, Elizabeth H., and Lauren A. Taylor. 2013. *The American Health Care Paradox: Why Spending More Is Getting Us Less.* New York: PublicAffairs.

Campbell, John L., and John A. Hall. 2021. *What Capitalism Needs: Forgotten Lessons of Great Economists.* Cambridge, UK: Cambridge University Press.

Chenoweth, Erica, and Maria J. Stephan. 2011. *Why Civil Resistance Works: The Strategic Logic of Nonviolent Conflict.* New York: Columbia University Press.

Cragg, Kenneth, translator. 1988. *Readings in the Qur'an.* London: Collins Liturgical Publications.

Curtis, Susan. 1991. *A Consuming Faith: The Social Gospel and Modern American Culture.* Baltimore, MD: Johns Hopkins University Press.

Daly, Herman E., and John B. Cobb, Jr., with contributions by Clifford W. Cobb. 1989. *For the Common Good: Redirecting the Economy toward Community, the Environment, and a Sustainable Future.* Boston, MA: Beacon Press.

DeMartino, George F. 2022. *The Tragic Science: How Economists cause Harm (Even as They Aspire to Do Good).* Chicago: University of Chicago Press.

Denis, Andy. 1999. "Was Adam Smith an individualist?" *History of the Human Sciences* 12, no. 3: 71–86.

Desmangles, Leslie G. 1992. *Faces of the Gods: Vodou and Roman Catholicism in Haiti.* Chapel Hill: University of North Carolina Press.

Desmond, Matthew. 2023. *Poverty, by America.* New York: Random House.

Diener, Ed, and Robert Biswas-Diener. 2008. *Happiness: Unlocking the Mysteries of Psychological Wealth.* Oxford: Blackwell Publishing.

Dorrien, Gary. 2018. *Breaking White Supremacy: Martin Luther King Jr. and the Black Social Gospel.* New Haven, CT: Yale University Press.

Edelman. 2022. "Edelman Trust Barometer (2021): U.S. Country Report." Accessed June 11, 2022. https://www.edelman.com/trust/2021-trust-barometer.

Ederer, Rupert J. 2011. *Economics as if God Matters: More than Century of Papal Teaching,* rev. ed. Lanham, MD: Scarecrow Press.

Eisenger, Jesse, Jeff Ernsthausen, and Paul Kiel. 2021. "The Secret IRS Files: Trove of Never-Before-Seen Records Reveal How the Wealthiest Avoid Income Tax." *ProPublica* (June 8). Accessed May 4, 2022. https://www.propublica.org/article/the-secret-irs-files-trove-of-never-before-seen-records-reveal-how-the-wealthiest-avoid-income-tax.

Esposito, John L. 1991. *Islam The Straight Path,* Expanded Edition. New York: Oxford University Press.

Fehr, Ernst, and Simon Gächter. 2000. "Fairness and Retaliation: The Economics of Reciprocity." *Institute for Empirical Research in Economics, Working Paper #40* (March). Also published in the *Journal of Economic Perspectives* 14 (March 2000): 159–81.

Feldman, Noah. 2003. *After Jihad: America and the Struggle for Islamic Democracy.* New York: Farrar, Strauss and Giroux.

Fisher, Jonathan, David Johnson, Timothy Smeeding, and Jeffrey P. Thompson. 2019. "Estimating the Marginal Propensity to Consume Using the Distributions of Income, Consumption and Wealth." Federal Reserve Bank of Boston Research Department, *Working Papers* no. 19–4. https://doi.org/10.29412/res.wp.2019.04.

Fleischacker, Samuel. 2002. "Adam Smith's Reception among the American Founders, 1776–1790." *The William and Mary Quarterly* 59, no. 4 (October): 897–924.

Frank, Robert H. 1988. *Passions within Reason: The Strategic Role of the Emotions.* New York: W. W. Norton & Company.

Frey, Bruno S. 2008. *Happiness: A Revolution in Economics.* Cambridge: The MIT Press.

Fukuyama, Francis. 1995. *Trust: The Social Virtues and the Creation of Prosperity.* New York: Free Press.

Gardner, Matthew, and Steve Wamhoff. 2021. "55 Corporations Paid $0 in Federal Taxes on 2020 Profits." Institute for Taxation and Economic Policy, Report (April).

Green, Michael, Jaromir Harmacek, Mohamed Htitich, Petra Krylova. 2022. "2022 Social Progress Index Executive Summary." Accessed November 13, 2023. www.socialprogress.org.

Gushee, David P. 2020. "Born in Heresy." *Sojourners* (Sept–Oct): 34–7.

Haass, Richard. 2023. *The Bill of Obligations: The Ten Habits of Good Citizens.* New York: Penguin Press.

Hacker, Jacob S. 2016. "America's Welfare Parastate." *Perspectives on Politics* 14, no. 3 (September): 777–83.

Haidt, Jonathan. 2006. *The Happiness Hypothesis: Finding Modern Truth in Ancient Wisdom.* New York: Basic Books.

Hand, Learned. 1944. "The Spirit of Liberty." Accessed June 9, 2022. https://www.digitalhistory.uh.edu/disp_textbook.cfm?smtID=3&psid=1199.

Hanley, Ryan Patrick. 2009. *Adam Smith and the Character of Virtue.* Cambridge: Cambridge University Press.

Hanley, Ryan Patrick, ed. 2016. *Adam Smith: His Life, Thought, and Legacy.* Princeton, NJ: Princeton University Press.

Haraszti, Zoltan. 1952. *John Adams and the Prophets of Progress.* New York: Grosset and Dunlap.

Hart, Stephen. 1992. *What Does the Lord Require: How American Christians Think about Economic Justice.* Oxford: Oxford University Press.

Hay, Donald A. 1989. *Economics Today: A Christian Critique.* Grand Rapids: William B. Eerdmans Publishing Company.

Heilbroner, Robert L. 1982. "The Socialization of the Individual in Adam Smith," *History of Political Economy* 14, no. 3: 427–39.

Held, Virginia. 1990. "Mothering versus Contract." In *Beyond Self-Interest*, edited by Jane J. Mansbridge. Chicago: University of Chicago Press.

Heyne, Paul. 2008. *"Are Economists Basically Immoral?": And Other Essays on Economics, Ethics, and Religion*, edited by Geoffrey Brennan and A. M. C. Waterman. Indianapolis, IN: Liberty Press.

Hill, John E. 2016. *Adam Smith's Equality and the Pursuit of Happiness.* New York: Palgrave MacMillan.

———. 2007. *Democracy, Equality and Justice: John Adams, Adam Smith, and Political Economy*. Lanham, MD: Lexington Books.

———. 2013. "Economic Justice, Laissez-faire Capitalism, and Political Islam." *Encounter, A Journal of Theological Scholarship* 73, no. 2 (Winter/Spring): 13–30.

———. 2010. "John Adams: Journey to Religious Tolerance." *Public Humanist* blog published by Mass Humanities (March 25).

Hogan, Margaret A., C. James Taylor, Celeste Walker, Anne Decker Cecere, Gregg L. Lint, Hobson Woodward, and Mary T. Claffey, eds. 2005. *Adams Family Correspondence*, Volume 7, January 1786–February 1787. Cambridge: The Belknap Press of Harvard University Press.

Hogan, Margaret A., C. James Taylor, Karen N. Barzilay, Hobson Woodward, Mary T. Claffey Robert F. Karachuk, Sara B. Sikes, Gregg L. Lint, eds. 2009. *Adams Family Correspondence*, Volume 9, January 1790–December 1793. Cambridge: The Belknap Press of Harvard University Press.

Horowitz, Sara, with Andy Kifer. 2021. *Mutualism: Building the Next Economy from the Ground Up.* New York: Random House.

Humphreys, R. Stephen. 1999. *Between Memory and Desire: The Middle East in a Troubled Age*. Berkeley: University of California Press.

Hutson, James. 2003. *Forgotten Features of the Founding: The Recovery of Religious Themes in the Early American Republic*. Lanham, MD: Lexington Books.

Independent Welding Distributors Cooperative. Accessed September 27, 2021. https://www.iwdc.coop.

Jackson, Dave, and Neta Jackson. 2009. *Living Together in a World Falling Apart.* Evanston: Castle Rock Creative.

John Paul II, Pope. 1987. *On Social Concern (Sollicitudo Rei Socialis*). Vatican City: Libreria Editrice Vaticana.

Kay, John. 2018. "Is there more to Adam Smith than free markets?" *Financial Times* (July 25). https://www.ft.com/content/1b9af120-890b-11e8-affd-da9960227309.

Kennedy, Gavin. 2010. *A Moral Philosopher and his Political Economy,* 2nd ed. New York: Palgrave Macmillan.

King, Martin Luther, Jr. 1958. *Stride Toward Freedom: The Montgomery Story.* San Francisco: Harper and Row.

———. 1967. *Where Do We Go from Here: Chaos or Community?* New York: Harper & Row.

Knowlton, Paul E., and Aaron E. Hedges. 2021. *Better Capitalism: Jesus, Adam Smith, Ayn Rand, and MLK Jr. on Moving from Plantation to Partnership Economics.* Eugene, OR: Cascade Books.

Krugman, Paul. 2013. *End This Depression Now!* New York: W. W. Norton & Company.

Lakey, George. 2017. *Viking Economics: How the Scandinavians Got It Right—and How We Can, Too.* Brooklyn: Melville House.

Langer, Ellen J. 2009. *Counter Clockwise: Mindful Health and the Power of Possibility.* New York: Ballantine Books.

Lao-Tzu. 2018. *Tao Te Ching*, translated by John Minford. New York: Viking.

Lappe, Frances Moore. 1989. *Rediscovering America's Values.* New York: Ballantine Books.

Lawrence, Bruce B. 1998. *Shattering the Myth: Islam beyond Violence.* Princeton, NJ: Princeton University Press.

Layard, Richard. 2005. *Happiness: Lessons from a New Science.* New York: Penguin Books.

Ledley, Fred D., Sarah Shonka McCoy, Gregory Vaughan, and AlEkaterina Galkina Cleary. 2020. "Profitability of Large Pharmaceutical Companies Compared with Other Large Public Companies." *JAMA* (March 3): 323, 834–43.

Lerner, Ralph. 1979. *The Thinking Revolutionary; Principle and Practice in the New Republic.* Ithaca, NY: Cornell University Press.

Lewis, Bernard. 1998. *The Multiple Identities of the Middle East.* New York: Schocken Books.

Lint, Gregg L., C. Joanna M. Revelas, Richard Alan Ryerson, Celeste Walker, and Anne M. Decker, eds. 1996. *Papers of John Adams,* Volume 10, *July 1780–December 1780.* Cambridge, MA: The Belknap Press of Harvard University Press.

Lint, Gregg L., Richard Alan Ryerson, Anne Decker Cecere, C. James Taylor, Jennifer Shea, Celeste Walker, Margaret A. Hogan, eds. 2004. *Papers of John Adams,* Volume 12, *October 1781–April 1782.* Cambridge, MA: The Belknap Press of Harvard University Press.

Lint, Gregg L., C. James Taylor, Margaret A. Hogan, Jessie May Rodrique, Mary T. Claffey, Hobson Woodward, eds. 2006. *Papers of John Adams,* Volume 13, May–October 1782. Cambridge, MA: The Belknap Press of Harvard University Press.

Lint, Gregg L., C. James Taylor, Robert F. Karachuk, Hobson Woodward, Margaret A. Hogan, Sara B. Sikes, Mary T. Claffey, Karen N. Barzilay, eds. 2010. *Papers of John Adams,* Volume 15, June 1783–January 1784. Cambridge, MA: The Belknap Press of Harvard University Press.

Lint, Gregg L., Sara Martin, C. James Taylor, Sara Georgini, Hobson Woodward, Sara B. Sikes, Amanda M. Norton, eds. 2016. *Papers of John Adams,* Volume 18, December 1785–January 1787. Cambridge, MA: The Belknap Press of Harvard University Press.

Lyubomirsky, Sonja. 2008. *The How of Happiness: A Scientific Approach to Getting the Life You Want.* New York: Penguin Press.

Mansbridge, Jane J., ed. 1990. *Beyond Self-Interest.* Chicago, IL: University of Chicago Press.

Marsden, George M. 1997. *The Outrageous Idea of Christian Scholarship.* New York: Oxford University Press.

Mayflower Compact. Accessed June 30, 2020. https://www.ushistory.org/documents/mayflower.htm.

McCarraher, Eugene. 2000. *Christian Critics: Religion and the Impasse in Modern American Social Thought.* Ithaca, NY: Cornell University Press.

McKibben, Bill. 2022. *The Flag, the Cross, and the Station Wagon*. New York: Henry Holt and Company.

McLaren, Brian D. 2006. *The Secret Message of Jesus*. Nashville, TN: W Publishing Group.

McMahon, Darrin M. 2004. "From the happiness of virtue to the virtue of happiness: 400 BC–AD 1780." *Dædalus* 133, no. 2 (Spring): 5–17.

Meacham, Jon. 2018. *The Soul of America: The Battle for Our Better Angels.* New York: Random House.

Mill, John Stuart. 2011. *On Liberty*. Project Gutenberg EBook.

Minowitz, Peter. 1993. *Profits, Priests, and Princes: Adam Smith's Emancipation of Economics from Politics and Religion.* Palo Alto, CA: Stanford University Press.

Mishel, Lawrence, and Jori Kandra. 2021. "CEO pay has skyrocketed 1,322% since 1978, CEOs were paid 351 times as much as a typical worker in 2020: Report." Economic Policy Institute (August 10). Accessed May 30, 2022. https://www.epi.org/publication/ceo-pay-in-2020.

Mossner, Ian Campbell, and Ian Simpson Ross, eds. 1987. *The Correspondence of Adam Smith.* Indianapolis, IN: Liberty Classics.

National Cooperative Business Association/CLUSA. 2021. Accessed October 29, 2021. https://ncbaclusa.coop/ncba-clusa-membership.

Nelson, Robert H. 2001. *Economics as Religion: from Samuelson to Chicago and Beyond.* University Park: Pennsylvania State University Press.

Noah, Timothy. 2022. "Is the Typical CEO Really Worth $15 Million?" *The New Republic* (May 17). Accessed May 26, 2022. https://newrepublic.com/article/166509/skyrocketing-ceo-pay-corporate-america.

Norman, Jesse. 2018. *Adam Smith: What He Thought, and Why It Matters.* London: Penguin.

Nouwen, Henri. *The Road to Peace: Writings on Peace and Justice*. John Dear, ed. Maryknoll, NY: Orbis Books, 1998.

Oreskes, Naomi, and Erik M. Conway. 2023. *The Big Myth: How American Business Taught Us to Loathe Government and Love the Free Market.* New York: Bloomsbury Publishing.

Organization for Economic Cooperation and Development (OECD). 2020. *Statistical Abstracts.* "Average Annual hours actually worked per worker." Accessed June 12, 2020. http://stats.OECD.org.

Ostry, Jonathan D., Andrew Berg, Charalambos Tsangarides. 2014. "Redistribution, inequality, and sustainable growth: Reconsidering the evidence." *VOXeu; CEPR* (March 6).

Ostry, Jonathan David, Prakash Loungani, and Andrew Berg. 2019. *Confronting Inequality: How Societies Can Choose Inclusive Growth.* New York: Columbia University Press.

Pangle, Lorraine Smith, and Thomas L. Pangle. 1993. *The Learning of Liberty: The Educational Ideas of the American Founders.* Lawrence: University Press of Kansas.

Philippon, Thomas. 2019. *The Great Reversal: How America Gave Up on Free Markets.* Cambridge, MA: The Belknap Press of Harvard University Press.

Phillips, Kevin. 2002. *Wealth and Democracy: A Political History of the American Rich.* New York: Broadway Books.

Piketty, Thomas. 2022. *A Brief History of Inequality.* Steven Rendall, trans. Cambridge, MA: The Belknap Press of Harvard University Press.

———. 2020. *Capital and Ideology.* Arthur Goldhammer, trans. Cambridge, MA: The Belknap Press of Harvard University Press.

———. 2014. *Capital in the Twenty-First Century.* Arthur Goldhammer, trans. Cambridge, MA: The Belknap Press of Harvard University Press.

Pregeant, Russell. 2023. *Converting Christians to the Jesus Ethic.* Eugene, OR: Cascade Books.

———. 2016. *For the Healing of the Nation: A Biblical Vision.* Eugene, OR: Cascade Books.

———. 2004. *Matthew*. St. Louis, MO: Chalice Press.

———. 2022. *Mystery Without Magic: Finding Faith in a Secular World,* 2nd ed. Anoka, MN: Process Century Press.

———. 2006. *Reading the Bible for All the Wrong Reasons.* Minneapolis, MN: Fortress Press.

Prindle, David F. 2006. *The Paradox of Democratic Capitalism.* Baltimore, MD: Johns Hopkins University Press.

Putnam, Robert. 2015. *Our Kids: The American Dream in Crisis*. New York: Simon and Schuster.

Putnam, Robert, with Shaylyn Romney Garrett. 2020. *The Upswing: How America Came Together a Century Ago and How We Can Do It Again.* New York: Simon & Schuster.

Quart, Alissa. 2018. *Squeezed: Why Our Families Can't Afford America.* New York: Ecco.

Rasell, Edith. 2022. *The Way of Abundance: Economic Justice in Scripture and Society.* Minneapolis, MN: Fortress Press.

Rasmussen, Dennis C. 2017. *The Infidel and the Professor: David Hume, Adam Smith, and the Friendship that Shaped Modern Thought*. Princeton, NJ: Princeton University Press.

Reich, Robert B. 2020. *The System: Who Rigged It, How We Fix It.* New York: Alfred A. Knopf.

Reichley, A. James. 2001. *The Values Connection.* Lanham, MD: Rowman & Littlefield Publishers.

Richardson, Heather Cox. 2023. *Democracy Awakening: Notes on the State of America.* New York: Viking.

Rosenblum, Nancy L. 2016. *Good Neighbors: The Democracy of Everyday Life in America.* Princeton, NJ: Princeton University Press.

Rosling, Hans. 2018. *Factfulness.* New York: Flatiron Press.

Ross, Ian Simpson. 1995. *The Life of Adam Smith.* Oxford: Oxford University Press.

Rothschild, Emma. 2001. *Economic Sentiments: Adam Smith, Condorcet, and the Enlightenment.* Cambridge, MA: Harvard University Press.

Ryerson, Richard Alan. 2016. *John Adams's Republic: The One, the Few, and the Many.* Baltimore, MD: Johns Hopkins University Press.

Sachs, Jeffrey D. 2008. *Common Wealth: Economics for a Crowded Planet.* New York: Penguin Books.

Saez, Emmanuel, and Gabriel Zucman. 2019. *The Triumph of Injustice; How the Rich Dodge Taxes and How to Make Them Pay.* New York: W. W. Norton and Company.

Samuel, Lawrence R. 2018. *Happiness in America: A Cultural History.* Lanham, MD: Rowman and Littlefield.

Samuels, Warren J. 1977. "The Political Economy of Adam Smith." *Ethics* 87, no. 3 (April): 189–207.

Sandler, Lauren. 2011. "The American Nightmare: We have everything the American Dream prescribed. So why aren't we happy?" *Psychology Today* (March 15): 70–7.

Schneider, John. 1994. *Godly Materialism: Rethinking Money and Possessions.* Downers Grove, IL: InterVarsity Press.

Schutz, John A., and Douglas Adair, eds. 1966. *The Spur of Fame: Dialogues of John Adams And Benjamin Rush, 1805–1813.* San Marino, CA: Huntington Library.

Schweitzer, Albert. 1949. *Out of My Life and Thought: An Autobiography.* C. T. Campion, Translator. New York: Mentor, New American Library.

Sen, Amartya K. 1977. "Rational Fools: A Critique of the Behavioral Foundation of Economic Theory." *Philosophy & Public Affairs* 6, no. 4 (Summer): 317–44.

———. 2011. "Uses and Abuses of Adam Smith." *History of Political Economy* 43 (June): 257–71.

Shain, Barry A. 1994. *The Myth of American Individualism: The Protestant Origins of American Political Thought.* Princeton, NJ: Princeton University Press.

Shorrocks, Anthony, James Davies, and Rodrigo Lluberas. 2020. *Global Wealth Report 2020.* Credit Suisse Research Institute.

Siblis Research, Ltd. 2021. "Total Market Value of U.S. Stock Market." Accessed January 22, 2021. https://siblisresearch.com/data/us-stock-market-value.

Siedentop, Larry. 2014. *Inventing the Individual: The Origins of Western Liberalism.* Cambridge, MA: The Belknap Press of Harvard University Press.

Skinner, Andrew Stewart. 1996. *A System of Social Science: Papers Relating to Adam Smith,* 2nd ed. Oxford: Clarendon Press.

Smith, Adam. 1789. *An Inquiry into the Nature and Causes of the Wealth of Nations,* 5th ed. London: Strahan and Cadell.

———. 1791. *An Inquiry into the Nature and Causes of the Wealth of Nations,* 6th ed. London: Strahan and Cadell.

———. 1982. *Essays on Philosophical Subjects.* W. P. D. Wightman and J. C. Bryce, editors. Indianapolis, IN: Liberty Classics.

———. 1790. *The Theory of Moral Sentiments,* 6th Edition. London: Strahan and Cadell.

———. 1976. *The Theory of Moral Sentiments,* 6th Edition. D. D. Raphael and A. L. Macfie, eds. Oxford: Oxford University Press.

Smith, Page. 1962. *John Adams*, 2 volumes. Garden City, NY: Doubleday & Company.

Smith, Tom W., Jaesok Son, and Benjamin Schapiro. 2015. *General Social Survey: Final Report. Trends in Psychological Well-Being, 1972–2014.* Chicago: University of Chicago, NORC.

Solimano, Andres. 2014. *Economic Elites, Crises, and Democracy: Alternatives beyond Neoliberal Capitalism*. Oxford: Oxford University Press.

Staloff, Darren. 2005. *Hamilton, Adams, Jefferson: The Politics of Enlightenment and the American Founding.* New York: Hill & Wang.

Stein, David E. S. 2008. "The Noun (ish) in Biblical Hebrew: A Term of Affiliation." *Journal of Hebrew Scriptures* 8, article 1: 1–24.

Stiglitz, Joseph E. 2010. *Freefall: America, Free Markets, and the Sinking of the World Economy.* New York: W. W. Norton.

———. 2015. *The Great Divide; Unequal Societies and What We Can Do about Them.* New York: W. W. Norton.

———. 2012. *The Price of Inequality.* New York: W. W. Norton.

Taylor, Adam Russell. 2020. "In our Flawed Democracy, Voting is a Renewal Resource." *Sojourners* (September 17). Accessed September 18, 2020. https://sojo ,net/articles/our-flawed-democracy-voting-renewable-resource.

Taylor, Robert J., ed. 1977. *Papers of John Adams*, Volume 1. Cambridge, MA. The Belknap Press of Harvard University Press.

———. 1979. *Papers of John Adams*, Volume 4. Cambridge, MA: The Belknap Press of Harvard University Press.

Terkel, Studs. 1998. *The Great Divide: Second Thoughts on the American Dream.* New York: Pantheon Books.

Thompson, C. Bradley. 1998. *John Adams and the Spirit of Liberty.* Lawrence: University Press of Kansas.

Traub, James. 2016. *John Quincy Adams: Militant Spirit.* New York: Basic Books.

Urbinati, Nadia. 2015. *Tyranny of the Moderns.* Martin Thom, trans. New Haven, CT: Yale University Press.

Vance, J. D. 2016. *Hillbilly Elegy: A Memoir of a Family and Culture in Crisis.* New York: Harper Collins.

Varg, Paul A. 1963. *Foreign Policies of the Founding Fathers.* East Lansing: Michigan State University Press.

Wallis, Jim, and Adam Russell Taylor. 2020. "The Next Part of the Race." November 19. https://SOJO.NET/articles/next-part-race.

Ward, Thomas J. 2007. "Adam Smith's Views on Religion and Social Justice." *International Journal on World Peace* 21, no. 2 (June): 43–62.

Warsh, David. 2006. *Knowledge and the Wealth of Nations: A Story of Economic Discovery.* New York: W. W. Norton & Company.

Werhane, Patricia H. 1991. *Adam Smith and His Legacy for Modern Capitalism*. New York: Oxford University Press.

West, Cornel. 1982. *Prophesy Deliverance: An Afro-American Revolutionary Christianity*. Philadelphia, PA: Westminster Press.

Westler, Brendon. 2018. "The Many individuals of the Liberal and Democratic Traditions." *Perspectives on Politics* 16, no. 3 (September): 755–59.

Whybrow, Peter C. 2004. "Adam Smith's American Dream, Time to Take Stock." *Psychological Inquiry* 18, no. 1 (January 1): 57–9.

Wight, Jonathan B. 2007. "The Treatment of Adam Smith's Invisible Hand." *Journal of Economic Education* (Summer): 341–58.

Wogaman, J. Philip. 2000. *Christian Perspectives on Politics.* Revised and Expanded edition. Louisville, KY: Westminster John Knox Press.

World Bank. 2021. "Market capitalization of listed domestic companies (current US$)." Accessed January 28, 2021. https://data.worldbank.org/indicator/CM.MKT.LCAP.CD.

Index

About the Author

John E. Hill is professor emeritus of politics and history at Curry College. He is the author of *Adam Smith's Equality and the Pursuit of Happiness*; *Revolutionary Values for a New Millennium: John Adams, Adam Smith, and Social Virtue*; and *Democracy, Equality, and Justice: John Adams, Adam Smith, and Political Economy.*

www.ingramcontent.com/pod-product-compliance
Ingram Content Group UK Ltd.
Pitfield, Milton Keynes, MK11 3LW, UK
UKHW041839031026
15587UKWH00002B/887

9 781666 946826